Previous page:
Portrait of Orozco c.1939
by Juan Victor Araúz

Acknowledgements

● The exhibition, with which this publication coincides, has been organised by the National Institute of Fine Arts (INBA) in Mexico; Fernando Gamboa, Director of the Museum of Modern Art, Mexico City, has led the team which has assembled this exhibition with the most able assistance of Miriam Molina, Director of the Carrillo Gil Museum of Art, Mexico City. It is a slightly smaller version of the larger retrospective exhibition of Orozco's work held in the Palace of Fine Arts, Mexico City, during November and December 1979.

This exhibition was assembled under the auspices of Lic. Juan José Bremer, Director-General, and Lic. Luis Felipe del Valle, Director of International Affairs, of the National Institute of Fine Arts, and has toured to Europe through the ministration of Lic. Rafael Tovar y de Teresa, Director of Cultural Affairs, the Ministry of Foreign Affairs, Mexico.

We should like to thank all the lenders to this exhibition particularly Margarita Valladares de Orozco, the artist's widow who made so many works, both from the estate and the Orozco Museum, available for such a long time. She has also most kindly written a short foreword especially for this publication. Also most helpful were Alfredo and Lucrecia Orozco, the artist's son and daughter; Lucrecia in particular spent much time answering my interminable questions and showing me the Orozco murals in Guadalajara. Also in Guadalajara Juan Victor Araúz, a close friend of Orozco during the 1930s and well-known photographer in his own right, was most kind in lending his photographs of the murals there.

Other lenders to this exhibition include Sr Luis Cardoza y Aragón, Sra C. T. de Carrillo Gill, Lic. G. Martínez Domínguez, Ing. Pascual Gutiérrez Roldán, Ing. Luis Espinosa Ulloa, Galéria Arvil, Museo de Arte Carrillo Gil, Museo de Arte Moderno and INBA — all in Mexico City as well as the Museo Nacional de Bellas Artes, Havana, Cuba. Others have wished to remain anonymous.

Much help has been given by the Mexican Embassy in London: H.E. José Juan Olloqui, the Mexican Ambassador, has given help whenever it has been needed. Sr Horacio Flores Sanchez, formerly the cultural attaché in London, played a decisive role in ensuring that this exhibition came to Great Britain. His successor Sr Lorenzo Lazo has continued to be of great help.

In compiling the catalogue Desmond Rochfort in London and Dr Laurance Hurlburt in Middleton, Wisconsin, have both freely given help — in their discussions with me, in their written contributions and in their loaning of photographs. Thanks should also be given to James Findlay, Latin American Archivist of the Museum of Modern Art, New York, who gave up much of his own time to complete the bibliography, as well as to Michael Nungesser and Olav Münzberg in Berlin who have worked together on the Preparatory School essay.

Valuable help has also been given by Heinz Spreitz, Director of the Leibniz-Gesellschaft, Berlin, who has made his extensive collection of material on Orozco available to me.

Also many individuals and institutions have been most kind in giving permission for the use of their photographs here and these are listed separately.

In Oxford, Deborah Langton has been tireless in typing and retyping of manuscripts; Graham Halstead and John Hoole have together designed the exhibition installation and Christine Newton has devised the lecture programme and audio-visual aids.

Help on particular problems has also been given quickly, willingly and freely by Olbeth Rossi in Mexico City, Clive Philpot in New York, the staff of the Canning House Library, Clive Challis, Julie Lawson, Michael Newman in London and Anne Pears in Oxford.

We are grateful for the enthusiastic help of Richard Hollis, the designer, and the staff of Lawrence-Allen, the printers of this catalogue.

Lastly, I should like to thank the institutions and organisations which by their direct or indirect financial help have made possible the showing of this exhibition in Oxford. They are: The National Institute of Fine Arts, Mexico City; The Elephant Trust, London; The Arts Council of Great Britain, London, which supports the Museum on an annual basis; and the Visiting Arts Unit, The British Council, London.

David Elliott
Director, Museum of Modern Art, Oxford

Published by the Council of the Museum of Modern Art, 30 Pembroke Street, Oxford OX1 1BP to coincide with the exhibition of Orozco's work, 9 November 1980 to 4 January 1981

The Museum of Modern Art receives financial assistance from the Arts Council of Great Britain

Printed in England by Lawrence-Allen Ltd, Weston-super-Mare, Avon

© 1980 Museum of Modern Art, Oxford, and the authors Reproduction of Orozco's own writings and works is by kind permission of the Orozco estate, Mexico

Layout: Richard Hollis
Editor: David Elliott

Photographs:
The Orozco Museum, Guadalajara, Jalisco, Mexico
Instituto Nacional de Bellas Artes, Mexico City
Juan Victor Araúz, Guadalajara, Jalisco, Mexico
Museum of Modern Art, New York, Eliot Elisophon
Desmond Rochfort, London, England
David Elliott, Oxford, England
David Scott, Washington, USA
Peter A. Juley and Son Collection, Smithsonian Institution, Washington, USA
Dartmouth College, Hanover, New Hampshire, USA
Pomona College, Claremont, California, USA

Translators: Jennifer Lanyon, Anne Pears, Olbeth Rossi, Monica Saenz, Maggie Torres

Plans: Peter Guy Tucker

This catalogue has been made with the financial assistance of the Elephant Trust, London

An exhibition organised by
the Ministry of Foreign Affairs
and the Institute of Fine Arts,
Mexico

1883-1949
¡Orozco!

M/ORO
CL
3/81

Museum of Modern Art Oxford
1980

Foreword

● In 1932, when my husband went on his only trip to Europe, he chose London as the first stop on his three month long journey (according to his autobiography). One of the reasons for this decision was his long-standing interest in seeing the sketches Raphael had made for the Vatican tapestries which are kept in the Victoria and Albert Museum.

And, I believe that José Clemente Orozco got some ideas from his visit to London (and especially its large museums) which would be useful to him in the mural paintings, in Dartmouth College, in the North American state of New Hampshire — the heart of New England — which he was in the middle of completing when he took this trip. In fact, not very far from the bucolic landscapes of Turner (which are exhibited in the London gallery founded by Sir Henry Tate), there is a painting of another British master which depicts the Final Judgement. Confined to hell for avarice, one of the many figures in the painting (easily identified as an ecclesiastical dignitary) clutches the money he had managed to hoard during his ministry.

In Orozco's paintings in Dartmouth College, there is no scene of the Final Judgement, nor are there figures of ecclesiastics. However, there *is* an image of another miser, eating money, which clearly reminds one of the figure in the picture. This is not surprising in the case of a muralist, given that one of his passions, when he himself was not painting, was in admiring the work of his fellow artists. This does not mean that he did not have many sources of ideas and conceptions of his own and a very personal technique, but rather that he was naturally subject, consciously or unconsciously, to external influences.

On the 23 February 1928 he wrote to his friend Jean Charlot about the exhibition of Spanish painting on show in New York:

'Goya for example, in a portrait which is there, 'PEPE HILLO' is not the Goya of the anecdote, but the Goya who turns the impasto of colour into a craft. It is Goya the worker. Here it is not a question of 'admiration', 'pleasure', or 'study'. No, here one can feel humility as before a storm, a star, or any other spectacle of Nature.'

It is natural that such a commentary on a work of art should come from Orozco, a man of sensitive spirit. More than a commentary, it was one of the greatest tributes that anyone has paid to the genius of Don Francisco de Goya. But be careful! For a Mexican muralist this admiration does not need a fire to activate it; a shooting star does not need to be illuminated.

That Orozco wanted to be himself (even when compared to Goya) is proved by his own words. He wrote the following to Lawrence E. Schmeckebier from Guadalajara (the melting-pot of his most loved works):

'For many, many years it has been a mystery for me why all writers compare me with Goya. Of course it is a great honour, but I am very, very tired of it. Apart from subject matter (20 thousand years of wars or more), I do feel, I do see that the similarity is the same as, for example, between an orange and a monkey (me being the monkey). Striking contrasts of black and white? and one fooling around with black and white produces necessarily striking contrasts, willingly or not willingly.'

For my part, I would like to emphasise the importance Orozco conferred on craftmanship in painting. In his panegyric on Goya, the worker amongst chromatic painters, he relegated the SUBJECT or theme to the place it belonged in the art of painting: it was a vehicle impelled by creative imagination and the skill of the one who drives it.

Margarita Valladares de Orozco

Translation by Maggie Torres

A Comparative Chronology

Orozco

1883 born 23 November in Ciudad Guzman, previously known as Zapotlán el Grande in the state of Jalisco, Mexico.
1885 Orozco's family moved to Guadalajara, capital city of Jalisco.
1890 The family moved to Mexico City. Orozco attended primary school run by the Escuela Normal de Maestros. Also applied to be a part-time student at the Academy of Fine Arts, San Carlos. Near his primary school was the printing press of Vanegas Arroyo, whose publications were illustrated by such popular artists as José Guadalupe Posada. He later claimed that he received his first artistic stimulus from seeing Posada work there. **'Posada used to work in full view, behind the shop window, and on my way to school and back, four times a day, I would stop and spend one or two enchanted minutes in watching him . . . This was the push that first set my inspiration in motion and impelled me to cover paper with my earliest figures; this was my awakening to the existence of the art of painting.'**
1897-1903 Orozco studied simultaneously at the Escuela de Agricultura de San Jacinto and in the Escuela Nacional Preparatoria (High School). At this time he lost his left hand and wrist in an accident.
1901 Orozco qualified as an agricultural expert.

Orozco quotes in bold type
are taken from his **Autobiography**

1906-14 Orozco began formal painting lessons in San Carlos Academy for Fine Arts, Mexico City. **'There was no charge for the model. There were materials, a superb collection of old masters, a great library of books on art. In painting, anatomy, perspective, and the history of art, the teachers were good. Above all there was unrivalled enthusiasm. What more could one want?'**
Met Dr Atl at the Academy who had widely travelled in Europe and spoke of the great Italian murals and of modern theories of art.

Sculpture room
San Carlos Academy
c.1915

Mexico

1880-84 Manuel González, President of Mexico
1882 Birth of Manuel Ponce (d.1948) Mexican composer.
1884 Portfirio Diaz (1830-1915) began his second term as President. Under Diaz the Presidency became like a dynasty and, in spite of constitutional controls, he remained in power until forcibly removed by the Revolution of 1910-17.
In the early part of Diaz's 'reign' Mexico benefited greatly from an unaccustomed political stability which encouraged economic growth. But this was at a cost. Foreign investors rushed to exploit Mexico's ample raw materials but this was uncontrolled by the Government and little thought was given to the country's economic or social welfare.
Diaz's social policies were formulated by a group of scientific, positivistic philosophers called 'los cientificos', one of its leading figures was José Limantour, Secretary to the Treasury.
1886 Guanajuato: Diego Rivera born (d. 1957).
1888 Railway line completed between Mexico City and Laredo, Texas — the shortest link to the USA.
1896 David Alfaro Siqueiros born in Chihuahua.
A time of economic expansion:
By 1911 there were 15,000 miles of railway track within Mexico. Between 1874 and 1910 the population had nearly doubled to stand at 15,160,000.
1900 First strike of oil.
But living standards for the majority of people did not improve. A twelve hour working day was usual with no time off at weekends. Infant mortality averaged 30 per cent. Under Diaz, the rich ranch owners (haciendados) began to appropriate free or common land and refused to let the peasant or the Indian use it. The haciendado became a great landowner and political chief; land, power and wealth became concentrated into a few hands.
1900 Oaxaca: Rufino Tamayo born.
1904 Augustin Yañez born. Yañez was one of the pioneers of Mexico's 'new novel'.
1906 Strike of Miners in Cananea, Sonora, brutally suppressed by the authorities. Reformist junta exiled in St. Louis, USA published the *Liberal Plan* which called for, amongst other things, freedom of speech and the Press; suppression of political bosses; secularisation of education; restoration of appropriated lands.
1907 Strikes: Rio Blanco Textile Mills; cruelly suppressed
1908 Rivera to Spain to study painting. Travelled widely through Northern Europe. 1910 returned to Mexico. 1911 back in Paris where he stayed until 1920.
1908 Diaz said that he would not seek re-election at the end of his term of office in two year's time. Opposition to his regime centred on the slogan: *'No Re-election'*.

The World

1883 Death of Wagner.
Birth of Kafka.
1879-83 The Great War of the Pacific. Caused by the expansionist ambitions of Chile, Bolivia and Peru.
1884 Britain: Gladstone's *Third Reform Act*.
1884-85 *Conference of Berlin*. Bismarck tried to ease world tension on partition of Central Africa.
1886 Abolition of slavery in Cuba.
1888 Abolition of slavery in Brazil.
1889 Brazilian Republic founded by army revolt.
1891 Brazil adopted Federal Constitution in *The United States of Brazil*.
1893 New York. June: a panic on Wall Street.
1895-96 major frontier dispute between British Guiana and Venezuela. Dispute settled by international arbitration.
1895-96 Armenian massacres.
1896 Abyssinians defeated Italian Army at Adowa.
1896-99 France: Dreyfus Case.
1898 Death of Bismarck. Spanish/American War.
Guatemala: Notorious dictatorship of Manuel Cabrera (1898-1920).
1899-1902 Southern Africa: Boer War.
1900 China: Boxer Rising. Death of Nietzsche.
1901 Great Britain: Death of Queen Victoria.
Cuba gains independence from Spain. New constitution (Platt Amendment) confirmed right of USA to intervene militarily.
1902 Britain, Germany, Italy blockade Venezuela: on issue of lack of compensation for injured nationals.
1904 USA: President Theodore Roosevelt announced that *'America is an international police power for the American Continent'*.
Ecuador cedes rights in Caquetá region to Brazil. Bolivia cedes Tacna, Arica and Tarapacá to Chile.
1904 Chile: Pablo Neruda born.
1905 Russo-Japanese War.
Revolution in Russia.
1909-1935 Venezuela: Dictatorship of Juan Gomez. Development of oil resources.

President Diaz
c.1913

1910 Orozco contributed a few sketches to an exhibition at the National Academy in honour of the Centennial of Mexican Independence.

1911 June: Orozco joined the strike initiated by the painting students at San Carlos. This continued for nine months and it was successful in securing the dismissal of the Director. A freer attitude then prevailed. Death of his father. Began work as a cartoonist for the radical newspapers *El Imparcial* and *El Hijo del Ahuizote*; both were to the left of Madero.

'I played no part in the Revolution, I came to no harm, and I ran no danger at all. To me the Revolution was the gayest and most diverting of carnivals, that is, of what I take Carnivals to be, for I have never seen one. The great leaders I knew only by sight, from seeing them parade through the streets at the head of their troops, accompanied by their staff officers.'

1912 Orozco established his first studio in Mexico City and worked on the series: **The House of Tears** — scenes from brothels in the locality.

'I opened a studio in Illescas street . . . in a neighbourhood plagued with luxurious houses of the most magnificent notoriety which sheltered "embassies" from France, Africa the Caribbean and North and Central America. Out in the open air the Barbizonians were painting very pretty landscapes, with the requisite violets for the shadows and nile green for the skies, but I preferred black and the colours exiled from Impressionist palettes. Instead of red and yellow twilight, I painted the pestilent shadows of closed rooms, and instead of the Indian male, drunken ladies and gentlemen.'

1913 Orozco moved to the city of Veracruz and at the ex Museum of San Juán de Ulua made large oil painting inspired by the retreat of the Spanish Army in 1822.

'There is no doubt that he [Huerta] was a monster, but in this he was no different from other Victoriano Huertas whose exploits fill the pages of history.'

The Calavera Huertista
Anonymous engraving
representing General Huerta
c. 1913

1910 Francisco Madero, a liberal, emerged as leader of the Anti-Re-electionists. He believed in political rather than social reform: *'The Mexican people do not want bread. They want liberty'.* Madero imprisoned by Diaz on eve of Election. Diaz's 'victory' proclaimed. On release from jail Madero published *The Plan of San Luis Potosí* declaring the election illegal and calling for mass civil uprisings on 20 November.

20 November: peasant uprisings took place in many centres. They were largely suppressed by Diaz's efficient para-military police, *The Rurales*, except in the North in Chihuahua where rebel Pascual Orozco gathered a large army which included the bandit Francisco (Pancho) Villa. They waged a successful campaign against Government troops.

1911 May: Rebels win Battle of Ciudad Juarez. Diaz resigned the Presidency. October: Madero elected President. Diaz: *'Madero has unleashed a Tiger. Now let's see if he can control it.'* Emiliano Zapata (1879-1919) rebel leader in the South asked Madero to restore the appropriated lands immediately. Madero would not agree. November: Zapata issued the *Plan of Ayala*. This withdrew recognition of Madero as President and asked that: 'the lands, woods and water that the landlords, cientificos, and bosses have usurped . . . will be immediately restored.'

1912 March: *The Plan Orozquista*; Pascual Orozco withdrew his support from Madero and re-iterated the demands of the *Liberal Plan* of 1906. Pascual Orozco marched on Mexico City but was stopped by the troops of General Victoriano Huerta. Also Felix Diaz, nephew of the former Dictator, staged a revolt with General Bernado Reyes. This was suppressed and both were imprisoned.

1912-13 Manuel Ponce called for a new national music; composed his *canciones mexicanas*.

1913 From prison Reyes and Diaz staged a coup. They escaped and for ten days Mexico City was in the grips of a violent and destructive Civil War, the *Decena Tragica*. Madero asked Huerta to fight on his behalf but after nine days of vicious combat, and under strong pressure from the North American Ambassador, Huerta changed sides. **Madero** was defeated, arrested and, shortly afterwards, **murdered.** Huerta was made President. But this regime was not recognised by the troops in the North. Venustiano Carranza, Governor of Coahuila and ardent supporter of Madero, refused to recognize Huerta and gained support from Pancho Villa in Chihuahua and Alvaro Obregón in Sonora.

1913: March: These three signed the *Plan of Guadalupe*. Carranza was recognised as First Chief of the Constitutional Army. In the South, Zapata also refused to recognise Huerta as he saw no hope for the restoration of land to the peasants. Both sides inflicted serious losses on Huerta who became increasingly dictatorial and relied on political assassination to stay in power.

1911 Agadir Crisis.
China: Revolution overthrows Manchu Dynasty.
1911-14 Great Britain: Labour unrest and serious strikes.
1912-15 The Balkan Wars.
1913 US troops intervene in Cuba.

Madero and followers
by Posada, c. 1911

General Emiliano Zapata
c. 1915

General Carranza
c. 1914

1915 Moved to Orizaba, capital city of the State of Veracruz under Carrancist control. Made cartoons and illustrations for the Carrancist newspaper *La Vanguardia*. Siqueiros was working as a military correspondent for *La Vanguardia* at the same time. Both Orozco and Siqueiros had moved to Orizaba at the suggestion of Dr Atl who was the editor of this newspaper. **'Trains back from the battle field unloaded their cargoes in the station of Orizaba; the wounded, the tired, exhausted, mutilated soldiers, sweating . . . In the world of politics it was the same, war without quarter, struggle for power and wealth, factions and sub-factions were past counting, the thirst for vengeance insatiable . . . Farce, drama barbarity. Buffoons and dwarfs trailing along after the gentlemen of noose and dagger, in conference with smiling procuresses . . . A parade of stretchers with the wounded in bloody rags, and all at once the savage peeling of bells and a thunder of rifle fire . . . "La Cucaracha" accompanied by firing.'**
1916 May: Participated in collective exhibition in San Carlos, Mexico City. September: Held first one man exhibition at the Libreria Biblos in Mexico City. Made wall decorations for *Los Monotes* restaurant, Mexico City.

Cartoon by Orozco, satirizing the failure of the reform parties, 'No Re-election' is invited by 'Effective Suffrage' to join him with the other ideals of revolution in a common grave
1915

1917 Made first visit to the United States: San Francisco and New York. US customs officials confiscated many of his paintings of low life subjects at the border on grounds of indecency.

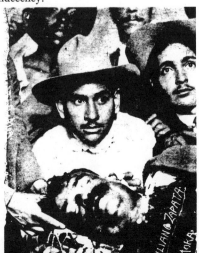

Zapata murdered
1919

1914 Octavio Paz born in Mexico City. The USA refused to recognise Huerta's Presidency and, after a minor diplomatic incident between the US Navy and Huerta's Government in Tampico, President Woodrow Wilson ordered his Navy to occupy Veracruz.
July: Huerta resigned the Presidency.
October: *Convention of Aguascalientes* called by Carranza to decide who should be the provisional President. Zapata's representative under the slogan *'Effective suffrage and no re-election'* recognised only Villa and Zapata as the true leaders of the Revolution. A serious rift developed between Carranza's supporters who favoured politically orientated solutions and Villa and Zapata's supporters who wished to adopt the agrarian reforms of the *Plan of Ayala*. No agreement was reached. Eulalio Gutierrez was elected President but was not recognised by Carranza, who then withdrew to Veracruz which the US troops turned over to him as a provisional capital. Anarchy followed and many atrocities were committed on all sides.
1915 Mariano Azuela (1873-1952) published *Los de abajo* (The Underdogs) a classic Mexican social novel. Orozco illustrated the 1929 edition of this.
1915 April: Battle of Celaya. Villa attacked Carrancist forces led by Obregón and was routed. Based on Europe's example, barbed-wire and machine guns were effectively used against Villa's cavalry.
October: USA officially recognised Carranza's regime.
Villa isolated in the North and turned his attention to raiding US border towns.
1916: March: Villa attacked Colombus, New Mexico. 18 US citizens killed. President Wilson authorized a punitive expedition to pursue Villa into Mexican territory led by General J.J. (Black Jack) Pershing. Carranza immediately asked Pershing to withdraw but he refused and the force stayed on Mexican soil until January **1917.** Carranza consolidated his position in Mexico City. November 1916 called convention of Constitutionalists at Queretaro. This continued into 1917 and resulted in the foundation of the **Constitution** which is still in force today. This was much more radical than Carranza would have liked: free and obligatory primary education; restitution of appropriated lands; only Mexican nationals to exploit natural resources; power of the Church restricted; 8 hour work day, 6 day week; equal pay for work regardless of sex or nationality.
1917 May: Carranza elected President: chaos — few of the articles of the new Constitution were implemented.
Carranza now moved against Zapata in Morelos.
1919 April: **Zapata** was lured to a meeting with one of Carranza's agents and **murdered.**
1919 Death of Amado Nervo, one of the most important modernist writers. His analysis of psychological problems was strongly influenced by the french realists, particularly Flaubert.

1914 Outbreak of First World War. Opening of Panama Canal.

General Francisco (Pancho) Villa at Aguascalientes

1915 Klu Klux Klan re-founded in USA.
1916 Sinking of the Lusitania. Battle of the Somme. Easter Rising, Dublin.
First free presidential elections in Argentina.
1917 Russia: October Revolution. Bolsheviks in power.
USA entered First World War. Sent troops into Cuba.
Third Battle of Ypres.

General 'Black Jack' Pershing
1917

1918 Germany defeated. End of First World War.
1919 Punjab: Amritsar riots and massacre. Germany: Foundation of the Weimar Republic. Spartacist Uprising. Murder of Rosa Luxemburg and Karl Liebknecht.

7

1920 Orozco returned to Mexico City and now built a studio in Coyoacán.
Third collective exhibition with the *Acción y Arte* group.
1923-24 Started first mural work at the **National Preparatory School** in Mexico City. Also working here were Rivera, Siqueiros and others.
1923 Founder member of the Union of Revolutionary Painters, Sculptors and Engravers. Married Margarita Valladares.
1924 Joined the staff of the radical newspaper *El Machete*. Forced to interrupt his work at the Preparatory School because of student unrest.
1925 Mural **'Omn* ** Mural **'Omniciencia'** in Casa de los Azulejos in Mexico City. Individual exhibition at the Bernheim-Jeune Gallery in Paris.
1926 Mural: **Social Revolution** in the Escuela Industrial in Orizaba, Veracruz. Resumed and finished murals at the National Preparatory School.

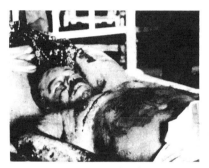

Villa murdered
1923

Siqueiros:
Study for *Democracy* 1923

1927 Travelled to New York and remained in the USA until 1934. Became friendly with Alma Reed and Eva Sikelianos. **1928** Group exhibition at the Art Center, New York.
October: one man show of drawings called **Mexico in Revolution** at the Marie Sterner Gallery, New York.
Began to make lithographs.
1929: 'The Crash. Overproduction and failure to export. World markets filled with goods that no one bought. Factories closed and immense negotiations at a standstill. Panic. Suspended credit. A rise in the cost of living. Millions suddenly laid off . . . Red faced, hard, desperate angry men, with opaque eyes and clenched fists. By night in the protection of shadows, whole crowds begged in the streets for a nickel for coffee and there was no doubt, not the slightest that they needed it. This was the Crash. Disaster.'

1920 Obregón now turned against Carranza and with a new Northern Army marched on Mexico City. **Carranza** fled and was **assassinated** on his way into exile. Obregón was elected President.
The Revolution now drew to an end; **between 1.5 and 2 million people had been killed in ten years of civil war.** Obregón created a portfolio for education and gave this job to José Vasconcelos, who immediately started to provide basic educational facilities throughout the whole of Mexico. In four years 1920-24 over 1000 rural schools were built also 2000 public libraries established. **Vasconcelos was also responsible for commissioning the murals at the National Preparatory School in 1923.** Rivera, Siqueiros and others were approached besides Orozco.
1923 Rivera started murals in the Ministry of Public Education, Mexico City. These were completed by 1928.
Pancho Villa murdered. Revolution against Obregón by Conservatives, the Military and Nationalists, led by Adolfo de la Huerta. The uprising was short but violent, over 7,000 were killed.
1924 January: Governor of Yucatán and champion of peasants, **Felipe Carillo Puerto assassinated.** Puerto was engaged to be married to Alma Reed, Orozco's biographer.
1924 Obregón handed over peacefully the Presidency to Plutarco Calles.
1924-34 Calles stayed in power for the next ten years, he started with liberal intentions but became increasingly dictatorial. Political prisoners proliferated as did political assassinations. Worked closely with Luis Morones and CROM, the leading labour organisation; Morones made Secretary of Labour.
1925 Philosopher Antonio Caso published *Principios de estetica*, an influential book stating that morality had to be based on sacrifice and love.
Manuel Alvarez Bravo made first photographic work.
Publication of José Vasconcelos's *La Raza Cósmica*. This emphasised the positive virtue of the Indian ways.
1925-30 Siqueiros abandoned painting to work politically with radical trade unions.
1926-27 Rivera worked on murals at Chapingo. Then visited the Soviet Union.
1926-28 The Cristero Rebellion. Catholic uprising against the anti-celerical enforcements of the Calles Government.
1928 Election: **Obregón** won but was **assassinated** before he had time to assume office.
Carlos Fuentes born, Mexico City.

President Calles
1925

1920 Geneva: Foundation of the League of Nations.
1920-30 Social instability in Brazil.
Siqueiros travelled to Paris. 1921 he was in Barcelona and published manifesto: 'A new direction for the New Generation of American Painters and Sculptors.'
1921 Rivera travelled from Paris to Italy and then returned to Mexico.
1922 Italy: March on Rome. Mussolini took power.
Provisional Government founded for Irish Free State.
Paris: James Joyce published *Ulysses*.

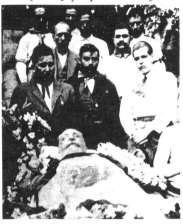

Carranza murdered
1920

1923 Germany: Hitler wrote *Mein Kampf*.
1923 Foundation of the Turkish Republic.
1924 Soviet Union: Death of Lenin.
Italy: Murder of Matteotti by the Fascists.

Diego Rivera at work
c.1923

1926 Nicaragua: Sandino's Revolt.
Great Britain: D. H. Lawrence published *The Plumed Serpent*, a novel based on his Mexican experience. This contained a description of Orozco's Preparatory School Murals.
1927 Soviet Union: Stalin became dominant in Russian Communist Party.
Chile: Dictatorship of Ibánez (1927-1930).

1929 February: one man show of oils and drawings, New Students' League, Philadelphia. Exhibition of Drawings at *Ferme la Nuit Gallery,* Paris.
March: one man show, the *Downtown Gallery.* New York.
April: Show of oils and drawings at the Art Students' League, New York.
1930 Feb: Inauguration of the Delphic Studios in New York with an Orozco exhibition organised by Alma Reed.
July: Edward Weston made portrait of Orozco.
Exhibition of drawings at the Albertina, Vienna.
Fresco mural **Prometheus** at Pomona College, Claremont, California.
September: murals for New School for Social Research. New York.
October: one man show in Los Angeles Museum.
December: group show in Delphic Studios, New York.
1930 - 31 An exhibition of Mexican art which included work by Orozco travelled round major US art museums.
1931. October: Group show, The Union League, New York.
One man show (lithographs and drawings) at The Wisconsin Union, Wisconsin.
1932 Started work on mural cycle at the **Baker Library, Dartmouth College,** Hanover, New Hampshire.
Later in the year broke off to make his first and only tour of Europe. This lasted three months and he visited the major Museums and galleries in London, Paris, Milan, Padua, Venice, Ravenna, Florence, Assisi, Arezzo, Rome, Pisa, Genoa, Barcelona, Saragossa, Madrid, Toledo, and Avila. Returned to complete Dartmouth murals by February 1934.
1934 One man show at the Arts Club of Chicago. Returned to Mexico City to execute mural **Catharsis** in the Palacio de Bellas Artes.
1935 Attended the Congress of American Artists held in New York as a delegate of the Revolutionary writers' and artists' League. Returned to Mexico and made **Suite Mexicana** containing ten lithographs.
October: Orozco's mother died.
1936 At the invitation of Evarado Topete, Governor of Jalisco, Orozco moved to Guadalajara to start work on murals for the Assembly Hall of the University. Title: **Creative Man and The People and its False Leaders.**
1937 Painted mural on vault over main stair of the Government Palace in Guadalajara. Title: **National Independence; Hidalgo; The Carnival of the Ideologies; the Phantasms of Religion in Alliance with the Military.**
1938-39. Worked on the complete mural decoration of the deconsecrated church of the **Hospicio Cabañas** in Guadalajara. Titles: **Humanity. Mexico before and after the Spanish Conquest. Man and His Quest for Improvement.**

1929 Election: won by Calles as eminence grise behind Pascuel Ortez Rabio the head of the National Revolutionary Party. Vasconcelos fought for election but was defeated.
1929 Martin Luís Guzman published novel *La sombra del caudillo*, a passionate condemnation of dictatorship and corruption.
1929 - 34 A time of increasing political control and repression in Mexican society. Support of CROM was dropped. More money was spent on armed forces. 1930 - 31 anti-Communist hysteria. Formation of the fascist organisation the Gold Shirts.
1929 Rivera started mural on main staircase of National Palace; also named Director of Academy of San Carlos. Painted mural in Palace of Cortez, Cuernavaca.
1932 Russian film director Sergei Eisenstein in Mexico filming *Que Viva México!*
1931 Siqueiros imprisoned for political activity.
1934 Lazaro Cárdenas elected President. Film: Ezequiel Carrasco's *Viva Mexico!* Mexican film industry develops.
1935 Carlos Chavez (1899 - 1978) composed *Symphonia India* and *Oberatura republicana*. Chavez studied the music of the Indian and incorporated their rhythms and melodies into his work.
Cárdenas was elected as a puppet of Calles but quickly began to establish his independence. His aim was to revitalise the Revolution and carry it further to the Left. He removed all Calles' supporters from the Cabinet and in 1936 **arrested and exiled Calles** himself. The agrarian reform programme was pushed forward and some 49 million acres of land were given back to the communities which had originally owned them.
More money was spent on education and health particularly in the rural areas but considerable successes were offset by a very large rise in the population. Organised labour was also strengthened and Vicente Lombardo Toledano took the place of the discredited Luis Morones as the head of the Confederacion de Trabajadores de Mexico (CTM).
1935 - 40 Rampant inflation: food prices rose by 49.39 per cent.
1937 Octavio Paz founded literary review *Taller,* publishing young Mexican and Spanish writers.
1936 Petroleum workers went out on strike for higher wages and better conditions. The owners refused to negotiate. Cárdenas ordered that the dispute be settled by an unbiased arbitration and this awarded a pay increase of one third and improved pension and welfare. The owners refused to pay and the result was that:
1938 Cárdenas signed a decree nationalising the holdings of seventeen oil companies. The USA protested but did not directly intervene.

President Cárdenas
announces the oil nationalisation

1929 Wall Street Crash; World Wide Depression. Trotsky deported from the Soviet Union.
1930 Coup in Argentina. Right wing government of landowners established until 1943.
Dominican Republic: Trujillo (1930-61) seized power.
Right wing coup in Brazil under Getulio Vargas. A fascist regime was established.
New York: October Thomas Hart Benton started Murals in New School for Social Research at same time as Orozco. **Jackson Pollock,** who had recently arrived in New York did action posing for Benton and **probably met Orozco at this time.**

1931 Rivera painted mural in the Luncheon Club of San Francisco Stock Exchange. Had one man exhibition in Museum of Modern Art, New York.
1931 Guatemala: Jorge Ubico elected President (1931- 44).
1932 Rivera made mural in Detroit Institute of Arts, USA using as a subject the Ford car works there.
1932 Outbreak of Chaco War between Bolivia and Paraguay (1932 - 35).
Portugal: Dr Salazar became Prime Minister.
USA: F.D.Roosevelt made President.
Siqueiros painted murals in Chouinard School of Art in Los Angeles, USA.
1933 Rivera started a mural for the Rockefeller Centre, New York, which was rejected by the patron. Rivera returned to Mexico in 1934.
1933 Cuba: US troops sent in. Termination of Platt Amendment by Cuba in return for trade agreement. Fulgencio Batista-President.
Siqueiros in Uruguay.
Germany: Adolf Hitler made Chancellor. Establishment of concentration camps at Oranienburg and Dachau.
1932 - 34 World Disarmament Conference.
1933 - 39 USA: the New Deal social and economic reform of Roosevelt. Many public murals by North American artists were commissioned as part of this.
1934 France: The Stavisky Case.
1934 - 45 China: The Long March.
1935 Italians invaded Abyssinia.
USA: Foundation of the Works Progress Administration under the New Deal.
Walker Evans, Dorothea Lange and others worked in the Mid West for Roy Stryker's Farm Security Administration.
Siqueiros set up his Experimental Workshop in New York which Jackson Pollock attended.
1936 Germany re-occupied the Rhineland.
Britain: Abdication crisis.
1936 Paraguay: Franco dictatorship established.
Bolivia: Toro dictatorship established.
Nicaragua: Sacasa overthrown by National Guard under Anastásio Somoza (1936 - 56).
1936-39 Spanish Civil War. From 1937 Siqueiros fought with the Republicans as a brigade commander.
1936 - 38 Purges in the Soviet Union.
1937 - 45 Sino-Japanese War.

1940 February: Cycle of murals on the Mexican Revolution at the Gabino Ortiz library, Jiquilpan. Michoacán, Mexico. June: returned to New York to paint the six panel mural **The Dive Bomber and Tank** at the Museum of Modern Art in New York.
1941 Executed cycle of murals in the Supreme Court of Justice, Mexico City. Titles: **Justice and false Justice. Proletarian Struggle. National Wealth.**
1941 - 42 Worked on a series of important portraits. From this time to the end of his life he made an increasing number of drawings and easel paintings.
1942 - 44 Executed cycle of murals in the Church of the Hospital of Jesus, Mexico City. Title: **Allegory of the Apocalypse in relation to Modern times.** This was never completed.
1942 Wrote autobiographical articles for the newspaper *Excelsior.*
1943 Founder member of El Colegio Nacional and had exhibition of work there. Installed etching press at home.
1944 Made a series of engravings, as well as many drawings and easel studies.
1945 Painted three murals for the Turf Club, Mexico City. Titles: **The Good Life; the other family of the Faun and Siren; The Feast of the Instruments.**
Worked on series of anticlerical and antimilitary paintings.
Exhibition at the Colegio Nacional called **Truth.** Returned to the United States where he makes a number of studies of New York life.
1946 Received National Prize from President Camacho for murals in the nave of the Church of the Hospital of Jesus. Made small mural, **Primavera** for private collection.
1947 Major retrospective exhibition at the Palace of Fine Arts.
Exhibition at Colegio Nacional entitled **Los Teules** (The White Gods). **1947 - 48** Murals in open air theatre of the National School of Teachers. Title: **National Allegory.** Also inside the hall are two murals. Titles: **The Defeat and Death of Ignorance** and **The People come near the Doors of the School.**
1948 Mural in the Sala de Reforma, Chapultepec Castle, Mexico City. Title: **Juarez, the Clergy and the Imperialists.**
1948 - 49 Painted vault of the Chamber of Deputies, Palace of Government, Guadalajara. Titles: **Hidalgo. The Great Mexican Revolutionary Legislation and the Abolition of Slavery.**
Made series of important large easel paintings.
1949 Started unfinished open air mural in the Miguel Aleman housing complex. **Died 7 September** in Mexico City.

1939 Siqueiros began work on Electricians' Union mural, Mexico.
1940 Presidential Election: Avila Camacho won. He was much to the right of Cárdenas and slowed down many of his reforming programmes. Inflation was endemic and in six years (1939 - 45) the price of food increased 2¼ times.
Mexico City: KGB agent murdered Trotsky in Coyoacán, Mexico City. A previous attempt on Trotsky's life in which Siqueiros had been implicated had failed.

1942 Mexico declared war on the Axis powers after Mexican tankers had been torpedoed in the Caribbean. Relations with the USA improved and many Mexicans now crossed the border to find work. The war period also considerably stimulated Mexican industry.
1945 Buñuel began to make films in Mexico.
1946 Miguel Alemán President. Cut back on military spending to less than 10 per cent of the total budget.
A firm base for continuing industrialisation was formed. But widespread corruption amongst senior government officials continued.
1947 - 48 Rivera painted Hotel Prado mural in Mexico City.

1938 Germany declared Anschluss with Austria and occupied Czechoslovakia. Munich Agreement: British Prime Minister, Neville Chamberlain declared *'Peace in our time'.*
1939 Germany occupied Poland. Great Britain and France declared war on Germany. Beginning of Second World War. Germany: by this time there were six concentration camps in Greater Germany. These were becoming increasingly used as extermination camps. By 1945 over 6 million Jews and dissidents had perished in these camps.
Great Britain: Graham Green published *The Lawless Roads* based on his travels in Mexico during the previous year.
1940 Rivera made mural for the Golden Gate International Exhibition, San Francisco.
USA: John Steinbeck published *Grapes of Wrath.*
Chile: Siqueiros working in exile after *l'affaire Trotsky.*
1941 USA: Japan attacked US fleet at Pearl Harbour. USA entered Second World War. Outbreak of fighting between Peru and Ecuador.
1942 Battle of El Alamein. Declaration of the United Nations.
1943 Right wing coup in Argentina.
1944 D-Day landings. Liberation of Paris.
1945 Great Britain: George Orwell published *Animal Farm.*
1945 Atomic bomb dropped on Hiroshima and Nagasaki. Second World War ended in Europe and the Far East.

1945-49 France: Jean-Paul Sartre wrote Trilogy: *Les Chemins de la Liberté.*
1945 - 48 China: Civil War between Communists and the Kuomintang. The Communists under Mao Tse Tung gain victory.
1946 Juán Peron became President of Argentina.
1947 France: Albert Camus published *La Peste.*
1948 Death of Gandhi.
Columbia: Assassination of Liberal leader Gaitán. Three days of riots.
Costa Rica invaded by Nicaragua.
1949 Great Britain: George Orwell wrote *1984*
1950 Outbreak of Korean War.

David Elliott

Orozco: a Beginning. 1

● In his autobiography, published some seven years before his death in 1949, Orozco gives us only the barest information about his early life. He came, it is evident although not stated, from a middle-class family and spent most of his childhood first in Guadalajara — the second largest city in Mexico where he was born in 1883, and then from 1890 in the capital itself. It was here that Orozco remembered his first contact with art. In his memoir he did not talk about the magnificent opulence of the colonial baroque churches in the city — full of sculptures, shrines and paintings which must strike any visitor, but rather of the memory of passing every day on the way to school the workshop of José Guadalupe Posada (1852-1913) which was situated in the oldest part of the city behind the cathedral, where he saw him working on crudely coloured and mass-produced broadsheets. Orozco described this experience as **'his awakening to the existence of the art of painting',** which perhaps is a little surprising as Posada was first and foremost a popular draughtsman; he worked directly with a burin on type-metal plates (later he used etched zinc plates) beside the shop of Vanegas Arroyo, his publisher. Posada was working in a genre — that of the broadsheet and chapbook — which had virtually disappeared in Europe and North America by that time. The combination of image and ballad in these ensured that his work could be appreciated by both the illiterate and semi-literate.

Posada outside his Mexico City workshop

Posada was a well known and respected popular figure — the master of a genre which had many practitioners; the public appetite seemed to be insatiable for new sensations. Such was his popularity that his work continued to flourish after the arrival of photogravure — to the Mexican people his drawings and caricatures may have seemed more real than photographs. It is significant that, with the benefit of

hindsight, Orozco saw in the work of Posada, the popular draughtsman, some kind of model for what art could and should be.

José Guadalupe Posada:
Revolutionary Calavera,
c.1910-12

But at that time Posada could not have been considered a serious artist. Mexico, like every other 'civilised' country had its own Academy of Fine Arts, but this, wholly in tune with the modernising and Europeanising spirit of the Diaz regime (1884-1911), looked to Europe, especially Paris, for a lead.

Whilst still at school Orozco enrolled in night classes at the Academy in San Carlos and there experienced to his cost the sterility of copying line for line, tone for tone, the lithographs of the famous French Academic artist Julien.

But at this time his family did not want him to study art and in 1897 Orozco went to the School of Agriculture in San Jacinto on a three-year course. Here he learnt to draw maps as well as the theory and practice of husbandry. He looked back on this time with affection and later wrote **'I had spent three healthy happy years in the country'.** He continued his education at the National Preparatory School hoping at that time to study to become an architect. He remained there for four years and during this time two critical events happened: firstly in an accident with gunpowder he lost the whole of his left hand and most of his wrist; secondly, his father died. The physical and economic pressures caused by these events must have been considerable: Orozco was crippled and could no longer count on financial support from his family. But his course of action was clear: **'my obsession with painting led me to drop my preparatory studies and return to the Academy . . . this time with a sure knowledge of my vocation.'** The death of his father meant that he had to take on work as an illustrator to pay his way through college.

Orozco started again in 1904 full-time at the Academy at a time when a new Director, Antonio Fabres, had just taken over. Fabres had come from Madrid and although his regime was based on the relentless and exact copying of live models and casts, this was enforced with the specific aim of giving students basic techniques and disciplines upon which they could base their later work. A new-found sense of energy and purpose ran through the Academy.

Little has been seen of Orozco's student work, certainly such discipline and his paid work as an illustrator gave him a valuable training for his later career. During these formative years he was also exposed to a wide number of influences which provided a critical and creative tension from which he could develop his own style. In San Carlos, as in any European academy, the foundation of drawing lay in the careful and exact transcription of plaster copies after the Greek and Roman originals in the cast room. The profound influence of this rigorous early training on Orozco can be clearly seen in the figure drawing in such murals as **Prometheus** 1930 (see p.47) itself a classical subject and in the three figures encircling the **Man of Fire** on the cupola in the Hospico Cabañas in Guadalajara (see p.88).

Yet besides this obvious influence there was also a considerable interest in new developments in Europe and these became known in Mexico in a variety of ways. Firstly, the Mexican artist Julio Ruelas (1870-1907), had absorbed the influence of European symbolist-romanticism. His work seems to have made an early impression on Orozco as did the whole *Modernista* movement as reflected in the pages of the journal, the *Revista Moderna* (1898-1911). Ruelas, influenced by both the Swiss symbolist Arnold Böcklin and the Munich painter Franz von Stück used classical forms in a strongly emotive and symbolist way; Orozco described Ruelas as **'the painter of cadavers, satyrs, drowned men and suicidal lovers'**. The *Revista Moderna* itself was rather less highly charged and was based more on the model of the French Art Journal *La Plume*: it illustrated, among others, Rodin, Beardsley, Japanese art and Art Nouveau and also promulgated the Symbolist/Decadent aesthetic belief that the work of art was, in itself, the expression of an idea: that is to say it *was* another reality and not a symbol or an allusion to something else.

The issue of the autonomy of the art work has been fundamental to the development of the art of this century and it is certain that as a student Orozco was well acquainted with these ideas. Much later in 1923 he wrote in a major theoretical statement: **'A painting should not be a commentary but the fact itself; not a reflection but light itself; not an interpretation but the thing to be interpreted'** — the work of art was for him the encapsulation of reality through the artist's will and technique. He rejected totally the idea that the work of art should be an illustration or even a narrative sequence. It was his adherence to this stance which was in his later career, to

distinguish him from other Mexican muralists such as Diego Rivera or David Alfaro Siqueiros and it is from this that his mature murals derive their succinctness and universality.

Another decisive influence on Orozco's work at this time was the painter Gerardo Murillo, otherwise known by his Nahuatl alias as Dr Atl (1875-1964) (*atl* was the Indian word for water), whom Orozco met as early as 1907. Atl had travelled widely in Europe, could talk at first hand about the wonders of the Renaissance and had a strong personality. He was older than the students at the Academy. Orozco remembered that he used to interrupt the students while they were copying from casts and '. . . **spoke in his easy insinuating, enthusiastic tone of his travels in Europe and his stay in Rome. When he spoke of the Sistine Chapel and of Leonardo his voice took fire. The great murals . . . Atl was drawing muscular giants in the violent attitudes of the Sistine.'** But, Atl was different from other teachers. He talked not about the mere copying of the forms of the Renaissance — but rather of capturing its spirit and energy. Atl's palette reflected the pure, unmixed colours of the Impressionists and his drawing was looser and more expressive than that of the students. On account of his greater age and persuasive personality he had a decisive influence on the history of the Academy during the Revolution. Orozco's own drawing style began to loosen up at this time as is clear from the few sketches that were published in the journal *El Mundo Illustrado* during 1906 and 1907.

Atl's overwhelming enthusiasm and rebellious nature served as a rallying point for the students at the Academy. He was able to envisage an art which was quintessentially American and which would rival in technique and conviction the best art of Europe. He was a stimulating teacher and encouraged his students to adopt a critical position not only towards the traditions within which they were working but also towards their role as artists within Society. In his autobiography Orozco captured the atmosphere of the many evenings spent in open discussion with Atl:

'In the nightly sessions in the Academy, as we listened to the fervent voice of that agitator Dr Atl, we began to suspect that the whole colonial situation was nothing but a swindle foisted upon us by international traders. We, too had a character, which was quite the equal of any other. We would learn what the ancients and the foreigners could teach us, but we could do as much as they or more. It was not pride but self confidence that moved us to this belief, a sense of our own being and our destiny.'

In 1910, Atl had organised an alternative exhibition of San Carlos' students work, which was shown in opposition to the official exhibition marking the centenary of the Republic. He was also successful in securing permission for the mural decoration of the amphitheatre of the National Preparatory School. Permission was given but revoked at the last moment on the outbreak of the Revolution.

Of course, previous artists, such as Leandro Izaguirre and German Gedovius had dealt with Mexican themes, but these had been historical subjects — an idealised Indian past — until then artists had refused to deal with what they saw around them. It was following Atl's example, as well as perhaps the popular influence of Posada, that in 1912 Orozco abandoned for a time the traditional subject matter of the Fine Arts to record the life of the pimps and prostitutes who lived in brothels around his studio in Illescas Street. There is little sympathy in Orozco's watercolours of prostitutes; the faces are masks — the bodies doll-like; the dark and emotive colours, small rooms and booths seem even more claustrophobic. Orozco watches this life from the outside — he emphasises its absurdity and lack of humanity; the automaton figures of the prostitutes and pimps are a parody of desperate, blind self-destructive forces. The figure of the prostitute also appears later in Orozco's work, most notably as La Chata (the snubnose —pp.70-71) in the foreground of **Catharsis** 1934 in the Palacio de Bellas Artes, Mexico City — a fiery and apocalyptic harbinger to the three Guadalajara mural cycles of 1936-39 (see pp. 72-89).

The Cinema, pencil, 1910-13 (cat.1)

Orozco called this series of watercolours **'The House of Tears'** (cat.4-14), the brothel was a house of degradation and suffering rather than enjoyment. In this, the earliest work to be shown here, there had been a considerable development from the earlier, more academic work and this may have been influenced, both in subject matter and style, by the work of such German illustrators as Karl Arnold or E.Thöny which was published in such pre-Expressionist satirical magazines as *Simplicissimus, Die Jugend* or *Pan*. These magazines would have been circulated around the large German emigré population resident in Mexico City.

But although now this seems to be the strongest work of this period, Orozco was also dealing with other subjects: he did many studies of young, pubescent girls. José Juan Tablada a poet and friend of Orozco wrote of these in 1913:

'Young women meet and kiss endearingly . . . furtive looks and affected gestures rehearse nascent perfidies, weapons are being tried out and sharpened for the coming duels of passion.'

These along with more general studies of popular life such as **The Cinema** (cat.1) are all made in pencil — and while they do not appear to be as compelling as the more expressionistic **'House of Tears'**, they do indicate yet another set of influences to which Orozco was exposed at that time — namely the illustrators of Parisian low life such as Steinlen.

Obviously at this time Orozco's obsession with painting was fuelled by a voracious appetite for all kinds of visual stimulus. Through European art magazines which circulated in Mexico City he would have been aware, although at second hand, of most contemporary European developments. He was able to transform these constructively in his own work.

The Meeting, watercolour, 1913 (cat.10)

The Hour of the Gigolo, watercolour, 1913 (cat.8)

The third kind of work that Orozco was making at this time, and continued to make until the mid-1920s, was political and social caricatures. It is here that the debt to Posada is most evident particularly in the humorous *calaveras* (skeleton jokes) which were traditionally prepared to be sold on All Souls Day — or, as it is better known in Mexico, The Day of the Dead. Orozco's first caricatures were made in 1911 for the two radical anti-Maderist newspapers, *El Imparcial* and *El Hijo del Ahuizote*. In 1915 he followed Dr Atl, who had just been appointed Director of San Carlos, to

Anti-clerical cartoon, c.1915

Calavera: The Merry Widow (and Cruel)
She has made the skull of her defunct husband
into a hatstand

Cover for magazine *ABC*, Mexico City, 1925
Caption reads: 'I bet I can take out your guts.'
'Not my guts! There's only marrow left.'

Orizaba in the State of Veracruz where he worked on
the Carrancist newspaper *La Vanguardia* which was
edited by Atl. This followed a pro-Madero line. In one
particularly disquieting front cover, sexual coquetry and
extreme physical violence are juxtaposed: the cute mask-
like face of a schoolgirl is incongruously framed by an
axe and dagger; the caption reads **'I am the
revolution, THE DESTRUCTOR . . .'** Even at this stage
Orozco combined opposites both in irony and as a form
of dialectic. An appreciation of this methodology is
crucial to an understanding of his mature murals.

In 1916 Orozco returned to Mexico City and had his
first one man show at the Libreria Biblos. He showed in
all 123 works divided into three sections: drawings of
schoolgirls, watercolours of prostitutes and caricatures.

After this exhibition it is likely that Orozco felt very
much at a loose end. The whole country was totally
dislocated through civil war and there were few
possibilities for working as an artist. It has been
suggested that Orozco now began a series of drawings in
pencil, ink and wash on the subject of the Revolution
but on documentary and stylistic grounds it now seems
likely that these were not made until the mid- to
late-20s. Even in the brothel scenes it was Orozco's
practice to observe first and then work from memory.

Dance of the Aristocrat, ink and wash,
c.1926-28(?) (cat.18)

La Cucaracha I, ink, c.1926-28(?) (cat.16)

The Field Hospital, ink wash, c.1926-28(?)

School as he was the equal of artists who had been employed there already.

The story of the Preparatory School murals is recorded below. These gave Orozco the forum he needed: he was to try first the genres of contemporary allegory and magnified caricature before making tentative steps towards a synthesis of feeling, truth and reality.

Orozco's mature images have a complexity of reference, a breadth of conception and an intensity of feeling which makes them remarkable.

In the Hills, ink, 1928 (cat.31)

Combat, oil on canvas, mid-'20s (cat.22)

In the latter part of 1916 he made a series of large caricatures on cardboard which were pasted on the walls of Los Monotes, a restaurant in Mexico City which his brother had just opened. At this time Orozco felt that he had reached a dead end; the horrible events of the past four years which he had directly experienced were still too close to allow for a positive reassessment of what direction his art should take. Tablada, in an interview not published until 1924, described Orozco's disillusionment with his own work at that time: *'If anyone speaks to Orozco in admiration of these paintings [the Los Monotes "murals"], he meets only a rebuff. Their creator is positive about the mediocrity of the wonderful figures.'*

The following year Orozco left Mexico and travelled to San Francisco where he worked as a sign painter and then to New York where he worked painting the faces of dolls. He returned to Mexico City in 1920 and made a scant living through his caricatures but his work as an artist was unacclaimed and unappreciated; it is likely that he did very little new work. It was not until the Northern American critic Walter Pach wrote favourably of him in October 1922 that there was positive reaction to his work. His friend Tablada also continued to speak out for him and was largely responsible for persuading José Vasconcelos, the new Minister for Education under President Obregón, that Orozco should be given the chance of making murals in the National Preparatory

Detail from the mural **The Reactionary Forces,** National Preparatory School, Mexico City, 1924

*'What does a man live by? By resolutely
Ill treating, beating, cheating, eating some other bloke!
A man can live by absolutely
Forgetting he is a man like other folk!
So, gentlemen do not be taken in
Men live exclusively by mortal sin.'*

Bertolt Brecht: *Threepenny Opera,* 1928

"Oh no!" said Kate in front of the caricatures. "They are too ugly. They defeat their own ends."

"But they are meant to be ugly," said young Garcia. "They must be ugly, no? Because capitalism is ugly, and Mammon is ugly, and the priest holding his hand to get the money from the poor Indians is ugly. No?" He laughed rather unpleasantly.

"But," said Kate, "these caricatures are too intentional. They are like vulgar abuse, not art at all."

"Isn't that true?" said Garcia, pointing to a hideous picture of a fat female in a tight short dress, with hips and breasts as protuberances, walking over the faces of the poor.

"That is how they are, no?"

"Who is like that?" said Kate. "It bores me. One must keep a certain balance."

"Not in Mexico!" said the young Mexican brightly, his plump cheeks flushing.

"In Mexico you can't keep a balance, because things are so bad. In other countries, yes, perhaps you can remain balanced, because things are not so bad as they are here. But here they are so very bad, you can't be human. You have to be Mexican. You have to be more Mexican than human, no?"

D.H. Lawrence: *The Plumed Serpent,* 1926

Such was Kate's reaction to Orozco's murals in the National Preparatory School in D.H. Lawrence's novel *The Plumed Serpent.* The book was published in 1926 and Lawrence and Frieda, his wife, must have seen the work just after it was completed. Kate was of course referring to the cycle in the first floor which Orozco put under the ironical title of **'Social Justice'.** The figures *are* gross caricatures: the discrepancies between rich and poor are shown graphically and clearly. The poor are parodied as much as the rich — the workers as much as the bosses. There is little sympathy evident for the underdog; the worker, the poor and the peasant are archetypal victims — exploited and manipulated. Such seems to be their historical and social function.

Orozco was neither a sentimentalist nor a romantic yet there is a fundamental human sympathy which runs throughout his work. Orozco's views about society and the role of man within it have often been misunderstood and the fact that he so often made his position clear through a series of oppositions, has led to the charge that he was confused in what he was trying to say. Orozco was unusual amongst Mexican artists of his generation in that he rarely published anything other than on art and he never joined a political party. Looking

back, his role in the Revolution was similarly equivocal. **'I played no part in the Revolution, I came to no harm, and I ran no danger at all. To me the Revolution was the gayest and most diverting of carnivals . . .'**

Similarly, he was equally ironical about his reasons for direct political involvement when he worked for the anti-Maderist newspaper *El Hijo del Ahuizote:* **'I might equally well have gone to work for a government paper instead of the opposition, and in that case the scapegoats would have been the other side. No artist has, or ever has had, political convictions of any sort. Those who profess to have them are not artists.'**

Admittedly, both these remarks were written some thirty years after the events described had taken place, but they refer to that very decade, the time of the Revolution 1910-1920, when the attitudes which were to shape the rest of Orozco's work were formed. Against the background of the thousands murdered and tortured during the Revolution, Orozco's comments could seem frivolous or in bad taste but, in fact, the opposite is true. The Mexican Revolution foundered on good intentions — on the firm convictions of those who knew what was best — and were prepared to die and kill to prove it. Orozco experienced, at first hand, the most foul atrocities perpetrated in the name of the most noble ideals.

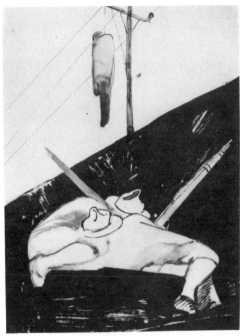

The Hanged Man
ink and wash, 1926-28 (?) (cat. 31)

During the Revolution all the rival armies, regardless of what they were fighting for, behaved with the same cruelty; as always it was the worker and the peasant who suffered. After the ten years of violent war it really did seem that the more things changed the more they stayed the same. Orozco's rejection and distrust of ideology could seem, against the background of the new developing Mexico of the 1920s, to have been politically naive. But many European writers and artists had experienced a similar reaction to the horrors of the First World War. Bertolt Brecht, for example, throughout the 1920s had a similarly cynical attitude towards human motivation — and a taste for caricature, but from about 1927 he began to follow Marx and so eventually the heroic transcended the cynical in the *Lehrstücke* (didactic plays) which he started writing in 1929. But Orozco did not undergo this kind of transformation. As in Germany, Mexican society had become polarised during the 1920s, particularly during Calles's near-Fascist dictatorship, but the lines of demarcation between right and left were less clearly drawn. Calles had the support of Luis Morones the corrupt boss of CROM, the largest union. In Mexico the Communist Party was not a powerful mass movement as in Germany. But the analogy between Orozco's and Brecht's approach to the broad humanitarian issue of man's place in society does not stop at their cynicism. Brecht, like Orozco, had a clear analytical appreciation of the diverse political and social forces which were moulding history. He communicated these points of view in his plays by the short episode — acted illustratively without emotion; the scenes would accrete

into an overall view — the play; the audience had to use its critical faculties to understand what they had seen. Orozco's murals also work in this way: they are a series of tableaux within the sequence of reinforcement and opposition which makes up the cycle. Orozco was often accused by the Mexican and North American press of being wilfully obscure; what did his images mean? He refused to explain — explanations too easily became substitutes for the work of art itself. We have already seen that Orozco believed fervently in the automony of art: its creation and its appreciation were essentially individual activities. It is this which distinguished his work from propaganda which aimed only to instil or communicate a direct, simple message which had a life of its own, independent of art. Orozco's works are many-layered and deal in a critical and sophisticated way with human issues; exploitation, corruption, cruelty and stupidity are exposed wherever they may be throughout society. Orozco was never prepared to let ends justify means.

Such an individualistic humanism won him few friends amongst Communist Party supporters. He was accused of not having a positive attitude towards the class struggle — of being a bourgeois sceptic — he was, they said, politically bankrupt and could suggest no positive course of action through which the masses could improve their conditions.

The 1930s saw a world-wide tendency towards polarisation in politics and society. It was the decade of the monolithic statement: the unambiguous exhortation to take one or another easily identifiable course of action. Orozco left, or appeared to leave, his options open. In the master works in Guadalajara, discussed in detail by Desmond Rochfort on pp.74-87, Orozco put forward opposing actual and ideal views of society and politics: in the University cycle false leaders exploit and oppress the people, yet above them, in the cupola, creative thought and action provide some slim hope of progress. In the Hospicio Cabañas the oppositions are less clear: we see as in the Dartmouth murals the panorama of American history: the Indian world, the Conquest, modern dictatorship. But the tone of the Cabañas murals is more despairing than those at Dartmouth; we see modern man governed by despots — he is divested by force of all individuality. The final image — the equivalent to the **Modern Migration of the Spirit** in Dartmouth (an enraged Christ destroying false idols) — is more illusive, more equivocal.

High in the cupola of the deconsecrated church is a man consumed by flames. Orozco characteristically never discussed what he meant by this: was it an apocalypse? — a punishment? — a cleansing? (of the Augean stables) — an abnegation of political action? This image is the sum of all these things — yet it is more than just a symbol or an allusion, it is both a prophecy and reality: for now have we all not seen, in our newspapers, a man of fire?

One fine morning in 1963, outside a pagoda in Saigon, a Buddhist monk became this. Soaked in petrol, he struck a match and set fire to himself — for an idea.

The first part of this text owes a considerable debt to David Scott's seminar article **Orozco's Prometheus** 1957

THE GRAVE DIGGER	THE MOTHER'S BLESSING	RETURN FROM WORK	THE MOTHER'S FAREWELL	THE FAMILY	RETURN TO THE BATTLE-FIELD	THE COUNTRYSIDE AND THE IDEAL
LAW AND JUSTICE	THE LAST JUDGE-MENT	LIBERTY	THE FALSE LEADERS	POLITICAL JUNK-HEAP	THE REACT-IONARY FORCES	THE REACT-IONARY FORCES	SOCIAL JUSTICE (2nd floor)
THE RICH BANQUET WHILE THE WORKERS QUARREL	REVOLU-TIONARY TRINITY	THE STRIKE Formerly (CHRIST DESTROYING HIS CROSS)	THE TRENCH Formerly (YOUTH-SPRING ZONTEMOC)	THE OLD ORDER formerly (STRUGGLE OF MAN AGAINST NATURE)	MAT-ERNITY	FOR IDEALS (1st floor) Ground floor

General view of
the north wall
of the main courtyard
in the National Preparatory School,
Mexico City,
Orozco painted murals on
all three floors
(see plan above).

Olav Münzberg and Michael Nungesser

The Preparatory School Murals, 1923-1926:
Between Allegory, Caricature and Historical Depiction

Total area 490 sq. metres

● The National Preparatory School 'Escuela Nacional Preparatoria' (ENP) in which José Clemente Orozco's first murals originated, houses the first experiments of the Mexican mural painting movement. It was here that the first collective attempts took place, building on European as well as indigenous artistic tradition, to find a new method of picture production which would be heavily influenced by the political changes of the revolution. The results give impetus to the forward thrust of twentieth-century realism. At the same time artists such as Dr Atl and Roberto Montenegro were making their own individual attempts at mural painting.[1] The murals were commissioned by José Vasconcelos who was Minister for Education. No conditions concerning what they should depict were imposed on the painters. They were free in their choice of motif and form.

The ENP was formerly the Colegio de San Ildefonso. It was built by the Jesuits in the colonial Baroque style and was completed by 1749. Since 1857 the building had served as a school of preparation for University study.[3] The building complex includes three areas of varying size: the Colegio chico, the Pasantes and the Colegio Grande.

David Alfaro Siqueiros (1896-1974) painted on the staircase of the Colegio Chico, Fermin Revueltas (1902-1935) and Ramon Alva de la Canal (born 1898) both worked in the entrance hall of the Colegio Grande whilst Fernando Leal (1900-1964), Jean Charlot (1898-1979) and Orozco painted on the staircase of the Colegio Grande. Orozco also painted the walls of the cloisters on the north side of the Colegio Grande. Diego Rivera (1886-1957) had been the first to receive a commission and he had started work on the adjoining auditorium 'Anfiteatro Bolivar' which was not built until the beginning of this century.[3]

These first pictures document the difficulties which Orozco experienced at the beginning of his search for a new means of expression in the years following the Revolution (1910-1917). Orozco writes in his autobiography: **Consequently, there was a time of preparation, during which much trial and error went on and the works produced were purely decorative, with only timid allusions to history, philosophy and various other themes'.**[4]

Orozco's early frescoes are mostly reworkings of traditional themes. They are hardly an accurate historical representation, nor are they convincing transpositions of a subjective viewpoint. Even Orozco began traditionally. Among these first murals the only one which exists in its entirety today is **Maternity,** the others were destroyed and overpainted by the artist only a few years after their genesis.[5] The inadequacy of these first works led him to this act of picture destruction. Orozco as indeed had Siqueiros, could not forget his experiences of the Revolution. But he was not able at this stage to translate his subjective feelings into new work, nor, did he wish to remain imprisoned in the objective allegorical straitjacket of his first murals. He had to resolve this contradiction productively by relating to the social changes of the Revolution and representing these in his paintings.

Orozco began work with an unhistorical abstract concept grouped under the general heading of **The Gifts of Nature to Man**; this contained paintings with such titles as **Virginity, Youth, Grace, Beauty, Intelligence, Genius** and **Force,**[6] of these only the realisation of the painting **Youth** can be proved.

The oldest extant mural is **Maternity** on the ground floor. In this the connection with the European Renaissance is evident, even though Orozco has transposed what might seem to be religious content into the secular sphere. The motif of the seated woman and child follows on from a long tradition of portrayals of the Madonna. The four hovering women, reminiscent of Botticelli, are equivalent to angelic figures. They surround a small boy who, like his mother, has been protrayed nude. The image itself clearly diverges from the portrayal of Mary with the child Jesus, but even the title of the painting, **Maternity**, indicates a more universal significance. In a country such as Mexico, in which the Catholic religion still plays such a dominant role, a painting of this kind inevitably made an impression which was secular rather than spiritual. The woman appears to the onlooker not as Mary, mother of God, but as a loving mother, a birth-giver whose nudity reveals her as a sexual being.

Maternity, fresco, 1923

The woman is blond, and light-skinned. She is holding and kissing the boy who is standing on her right thigh. The classicism of her head is in marked contrast to the particularly expressive gesture of the kiss. A robe covers the woman's hair like a hood and spreads down behind her body; its shape is like a pyramid or mountain and its tapering form suggests both earthiness and spaciousness. At the woman's feet a nude female figure lies with her back to the onlooker. She is holding some grapes in front of her mouth: this could be taken either as an allusion to the Christian belief that in the magical act of transubstantiation wine turns into the blood of Christ, or to the pagan idea that Autumn, the period of the wine harvest, was a time of fertility in the yearly cycle. Such a view is reinforced by the fact that one of the destroyed murals had the title **Spring** and this could have been linked to it.

Reading the frescoes on the ground floor of the main courtyard from left to right, **Maternity** now forms the conclusion of a series. After the paintings **The Trench** and **Destruction of the Old Order**, both made three years later, it stands for hope in a new order. A new society grows out of the ruins of revolution and war. The painting's dominant reddish-brown colour recalls the flames of destruction, but one is also aware of newly germinated life thrusting itself upwards.

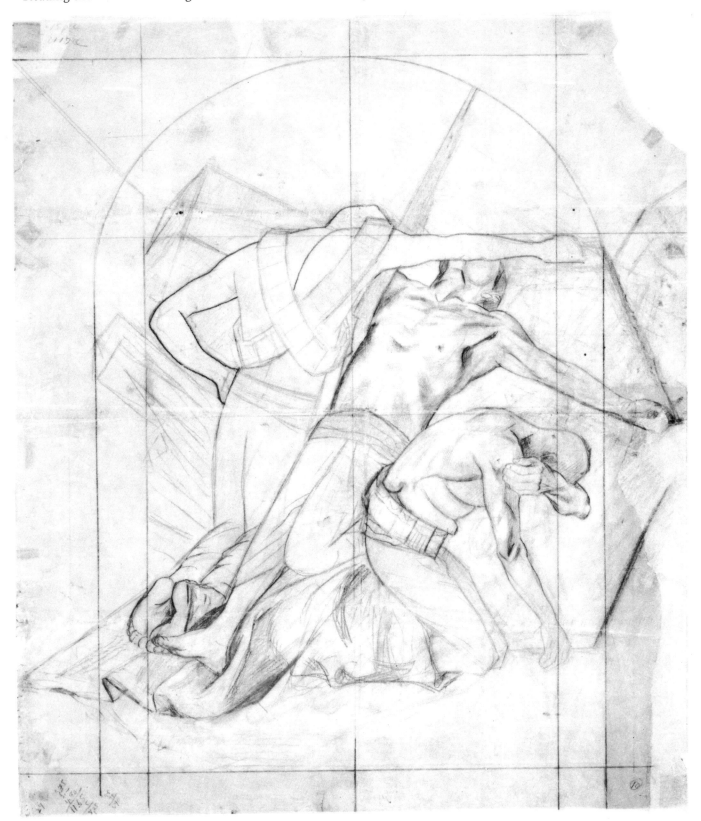

Study for **The Trench**, pencil, 1926

The painting can be read in a number of ways — as an allegory, a myth or even as a straight representation. But it is strange that Orozco chose to depict a blonde female nude in a country which consists mainly of dark-haired Indians and Mestizos; there would have been few possibiliities for self-identification. Equally puzzling is the dichotomy between the everyday nature of the mother-child relationship and the hovering female figures which connote an extraordinary event. These Christian components have not yet been fully reconciled in a new humanistic interpretation.

Apart from the painting **Maternity** only fragments of the original seven-part conception were ever realised.[7]

Above: **Spring,** fresco (destroyed), 1923

Tzontemóc, fresco (destroyed), 1923

The degree to which Orozco experimented is indicated in the painting **Youth** which should have formed the centrepiece and which protrayed a group of school girls combined with an allegory of the sun. It was renamed **Spring** after partial over-painting, and then was

completely over-painted again and entitled **Tzontemóc**, the Sun God from Nahuatl-mythology.[8] This painting shows an enormous nude male figure plunging downwards — the personification of the setting sun. But, late in 1926, Orozco also destroyed this painting and replaced it with the motif **The Trench**. This now constitutes the final version and can still be seen there.

The Struggle of Man Against Nature
fresco (destroyed), 1923

To the right of this, but to the left of **Maternity** was **The Struggle of Man Against Nature** which he replaced in 1926 with **Destruction of the Old Order**.[9] Whilst on the left he painted **Christ Destroying His Cross**, a motif which was treated many times, which he replaced in 1926 by the painting **The Strike**. In the new painting only the head of Christ remained. This large isolated head is placed on the uppermost edge of the door frame of a house. It seems, in the context of the strike theme, either to symbolise the head of a strike victim, or because of its halo, the head of Christ — an inspiration to the strikers who are putting up their red strike banner on the door of the house.[10]

To what extent the overpainted pictures can be seen as an expression of Orozco's original concept is not clear. The first paintings are characterised by stereometric and geometric forms: cones, circles and triangles. Such forms can be seen in the background of the much later painting **Destruction of the Old Order**, but in this they have taken on a new significance as they form the facades of houses. It is strange that Orozco has decided that these symbols of the Old Order should appear to be tumbling down as a result of some natural disaster — a volcano or earthquake — rather than, as suggested in the other paintings, by the revolutionary effect of new social forces.

Orozco's very first paintings aroused protests from a conservative Catholic womens' group, but it should not be assumed that this had any part in his deciding to overpaint them at a later date.[11] On the contrary, the protest of these women, who during a charity bazaar in the courtyard, furiously nailed flags, branches and garlands over the walls, led Orozco to capture their **'triumphant profiles'** [12] in a series of caricatures on the first floor of the main courtyard all of which were centred on the theme of social justice.

If the allegorical language and geometric forms of the first paintings signified a secular break with previous Catholic-dominated, Mexican iconography, so the paintings which followed, both the first substitutes and those made later, show a breakthrough towards the use of social motifs and a more formal language. This

The Strike, fresco, 1926

Christus Destroying His Cross,
fresco (destroyed), 1923

corresponded not only with the painter's own experience, but also with what actually happened; it showed his reaction to the rifts in society caused by the Revolution, the march forward into a new society and the clearing away of the last remnants of feudalism. Reflecting this he painted such images as the **Revolutionary Trinity** in which workers, farmers and soldiers, and their relationship to each other, are defined in an analytical way. It is a painting which is related on the one hand to the iconology and iconography of the Russian October Revolution, and on the other hand looks back to the Christian Trinity — remodelled and secularised. This is even more evident in the adjacent panel **The Rich Banquet while the Workers Quarrel** in which Christian iconography has been dispensed with altogether to be replaced by an iconography of class.[13] This theme is continued in **The Trench.**

In this painting, the death of a revolutionary is equated with the crucifixion of Christ. The middle figure, who is lying on his back with his left arm extended on a barricade, seems to be stretched out as on a cross. His body, the slanted rifle and the body of the figure to his left, who is falling onto him, form the upright and one diagonal. Orozco portrays three revolutionaries one of whom is hiding his face in agony. The wasted bodies of the fighters, painted in brown, earthy colours, suffused with blood red, seem massive. The horizon is bathed in deep red, but, it is not clear whether it is sunrise or sunset; such an obvious allusion would have cheapened the scene. Nor can the red be directly understood as the glow of a fire. His choice of colour and portrayal of form stem from an expressionistic realism which uses symbolic illusion in a manner not unlike Max Beckmann. This heightened realism conveys rather than portrays Orozco's inner relationship to the Revolution, which in this case is not transfigured or idealised as, for example, in the pictures of Delacroix. Orozco concentrates on the suffering which Revolution brings in its path, but he stands well back from the pathos which is an integral part of it. Despite his affirmation of the Revolution, Orozco retreats in the face of the futility of such suffering by allusion to the futility of Christ's sacrificial death in this work.[14] The use of such imagery could suggest that Orozco was disillusioned or sceptical.

The **Revolutionary Trinity** which is on the same floor as **The Trench** is celebrated by the Mexican art critic Antonio Rodrigues as the painting *'in which the Mexico of strife and bloodshed makes its solemn and dramatic entry into the domain of mural painting.'* [15] In the painting Orozco shows that the union of workers, farmers and soldiers is not working in Mexico. On the left a farmer kneels, his hands folded together, obscuring his face, on the right a worker, with only stumps for arms directs his startled and angry gaze at the armed figure in the middle: a soldier whose face is concealed by a flag which swells to form an outsize Jacobin cap.[16]

If **The Revolutionary Trinity** is read in conjunction with **The Rich Banquet while the Poor Quarrel** it becomes obvious that the soldier is at the same height as the table of the rich and thus belongs to their sphere. If one accepts this kind of correspondence, the soldier is, at the behest of the bourgeoisie, dividing by force the developing unity of the farmers and workers by walking between their ranks and forcing them to their knees, while, in the adjacent panel to the left, sections of the working class are being torn apart by internal strife. The soldier embodies the brutality of the pseudo-revolutionary state powers. The picture of the **The Revolutionary Trinity** as we see it today is an intensification of Orozco's first version of the subject,[17] in which the worker's head and attitude were identical, but, instead of stumps he had healthy arms. He was holding a screwdriver and a drill. In place of the farmer there was an engineer.

The first floor, entitled **Social Justice,** which Orozco painted from 1923 until he broke off against his will in 1924, contains a number of caricatures which do not have to be read in a set sequence.[18] From left to right they are: **The Reactionary Forces, The Money Box, Political Junkheap, The False Leaders, Liberty, The Last Judgement** and **Law and Justice**.

In **The Reactionary Forces** aristocrats and bourgeois walk past the poor sitting by the roadside and asking in vain for alms. They walk in a procession towards the church door. The exaggerated dimensions of the rich find their counterpoint in the reduced dimensions of those seated. Orozco's attack is directed at both: against the unnatural subservience of the poor and against the similarly unnatural arrogance of the rich which conceals their self-deception and social amorality.

The next image is over a window; it is an offertory box into which money is being given from both sides by disembodied hands. It is clear from the ragged covering on these arms that the donors are poor people. In **Political Junkheap** various symbols of power have been collected together on a rubbish heap: crowns, lances, episcopal crooks, bound rods — the fasces

Political Junkheap, fresco, 1924

(symbols of Italian Fascism) and the swastika, which even at this time was taken by Orozco to be a negative symbol of power and terror. Orozco has also thrown the red Jacobin cap onto the rubbish heap of history.

In the next painting **The False Leaders** Orozco criticizes the complicity of the clergy with secular power. A big-bellied figure leads the way: he belongs to the propertied classes and is characterised as a false liberator. On his head he wears something like a crown of thorns — a suggestion of sacrifice and martyrdom; he holds in one hand a Jacobin cap as if it were a glove puppet — a symbol of temptation and seduction and a black and red flag in the other. Between this figure and that of a masked priest stands a grotesque figure holding a shovel in one hand and the black and red flag of anarchy in the other. The priest is about to stab him in the back with a curved knife. This contrived figure embodies the position of the workers and the farmers caught between the twin powers of Church and State. The Jacobin cap recurs in the next painting **Liberty** an allusion to the symbol of the French Revolution. But she is portrayed as an ugly, pimply old woman hovering over a window frame; she is like a puppet who is hoisted above the stage of world history by fraying ropes.

The central theme of **Social Justice** is stated particularly clearly in the frescoes **The Last Judgement** and **Law and Justice** on the extreme left. Here divine and wordly justice are caricatured; one by an exaggerated and wrathful figure of God the Father, the other by a drunken pair in carnival costume.

The murals on both the ground floor and first floor led at the end of June 1924 to public rioting by groups of conservative students.[19] This resulted in the interruption of work in the ENP, the dismissal of Orozco — as well as of Siqueiros who was painting on the stairs of the Colegio chico — and to a petty demand for the repayment of fees for the rather spurious reason that the time limit for their completion had been passed. Orozco was not able to resume work in the ENP until 1926. The murals had been commissioned by the State and had come into being under its protection, when this was withdrawn the mural painting could not continue. The students mutilated some frescoes by scratching slogans and lines on the pictures. Supported by a conservative press which accused the painter of 'deviation from beauty' they spoke of 'apocalyptic monsters' and of the ridiculing of Mexico. This destruction was made possible by a general public climate of intolerance and by the apparently imminent resignation of Vasconcelos. Orozco sought to rally public support through a petition which was put up as a

Left, detail from **The Reactionary Forces,** fresco, 1924
Below, study **The Reactionary Forces,** pencil, 1924

Cortez and Malinche
fresco, 1926
Right:
The Friar and the Indian,
fresco 1926

Liberty and **The False Leaders,** 1924, general view

Detail from **The False Leaders** 1924

poster and also printed in the press, as well as from an initiative by the North-American writers Anita Brenner and Carlton Beals. Besides this the Artists' Union also published a protest.[20]

The walls on the second floor were not painted until 1926.[21] But Orozco painted two murals on other sites in the meantime; one, in Mexico — entitled **Omniscience** which was completed in the Casa de Azulejos in Mexico City in 1925, the other in 1926 in the then industrial school in Orizaba in the state of Veracruz, with the title **Social Revolution**. In the same year he received permission from the national university to continue the murals in the ENP.[22]

The murals on the second floor deal with the effects of the Revolution in the country at that time.[23] In these, Orozco's own feelings of sorrow and regret are evident. A plough stands unused. Its owner is dead or has been drawn into the Civil War. Scenes of departure. The grave-digger with a dreamy, youthful face is having a rest and falls into the grave he is digging. A farm is on fire. Farmers return from their work in the fields. Revolutionaries are leaving the village. These scenes have no chronological structure, but show a simultaneity of events. The simplicity of the representation which characterises these paintings is not be employed again by Orozco except possibly in the New School Murals. Nor does he show again in a mural his sympathy with country people. He will concentrate on allegorical or symbolical themes and directs his own

criticisms against the aggression of an unjust world. The formal language on the second floor is also seen in two paintings **Thirst** and **Engineers** which were painted as panels on both sides of the entry to the staircase to the upper storeys.[24]

The murals in the School courtyard give a retrospective indication of Orozco's own position towards the Revolution. These, rather than any verbal statement, give the clearest indication of what this was. Although he sarcastically states in his autobiography that the Revolution had been for him '**the gayest and most diverting of carnivals**', such levity is not to be found in the formal language of his paintings.[25] Such statements, however, underline Orozco's deep ambivalence towards Revolution; it awakes hopes but soon sinks into failure; huge forces of energy are liberated but to achieve meagre results. Antonio Rodriguez wrote '*He — [Orozco] did not glorify revolution. He was sincere in saying that great social phenomena need no glorification. Whenever he painted revolutionary scenes, he did it in the black and red of his colourful idiom, but he did it in all seriousness, as if showing the midnight struggle of the sun, which enables it to re-appear next day to give light to the earth. If Orozco does not extol the Revolution, he fulfils himself through it. How could we understand the Orozco of* **The Trench, The Soldiers** *or the* **Farewell** *without the Revolution? Diego Rivera idealised it: Orozco showed its greatness and its tragedy. The one was its singer, the other its interpreter. Both were its inspired "Tlacuilos"*'[26] Orozco's paintings on the staircase which he painted last of all in 1926 form a thematic caesura. In El Greco-like darkness of colours and forms, just as J.Charlot, R.Alva de Canal and E.Garcia Cahera had previously, he deals with the historical theme of the Conquest. According to one view the Conquest brought civilisation to the country after inhumanity and destruction. This position stresses the inhumanity of the early cultures, the cult of human sacrifice — and tends to play down or suppress the inhumanity of the Conquest itself. Another stresses the opposite: it idealises the early cultures and pays little heed to any civilising effects of the Conquest. A third standpoint lies in a compromise between the two poles.

Several frescoes were produced by Orozco which did not form part of any particular concept: for example **Cortez and Malinche**, **The Conqueror-Builder and the Indian Worker**, **The Old Warrior Races** and three different portrayals of **Franciscans** in charitable attitudes. In the Franciscan panels a friar is distributing alms and alleviating pain, another is clasping an Indian to him, a third is crouched over an Indian. In the painting **The Old Warrior Races** it must be left open as to whether Orozco is in fact portraying a violent struggle between Indians or violence suffered by them. The title of the painting does not help for as is so often the case it was not given by Orozco, but the source of the violence is directly visible in the painting. An Indian is lying in the foreground, over him is an Indian holding his fist clenched; this gesture is ambivalent, we do not know whether it

The Return from Work, fresco, 1926

Detail from **The Women of the Workers,** fresco, 1926

represents victory over or solidarity with the fallen Indian. In the murals **Cortez and Malinche** and the portrayals of the **Franciscans** Orozco shows secular and clerical power in relation to the early cultures. Cortez appears to the native inhabitants as a white hero or Christ-like power figure with Malinche — a symbolic figure of collaboration. With an aggressive imperialist gesture Cortez is either preventing Malinche from an act of mercy towards an Indian lying on the ground, or is separating her finally from her former life. He holds the Indian down with his right foot; the Indian lies next to an open grave, an expression of the historical demise of the early cultures.

In one of the Franciscan scenes the monk, dressed in a billowing cowl, does not step towards the Indian in an open way; he approaches him not as one equal facing another but as a superpowerful, all engulfing force consuming the naked wasted body of the Indian who kneeling under his weight is irresistably pushed backwards. The scene is again ambivalent: on the one hand the friar seems to be making a gesture of reconciliation, a brotherly kiss, but on the other hand his posture seems to clarify the true power relationship between them. Common to both pictures is the fact that the relationships portray either a latent or a manifest sexuality. The relationship of secular power to the early cultures is seen as heterosexual that of clerical power as homosexual. Orozco is playing on a marriage-like union in **Cortez and Malinche.**[27] He represents them simultaneously as a bridal pair and as a ruling partnership. A union reinforced by a hand-shake, if also involving massive compulsion. Similarly the role which Malinche played for many tribes confirms this: she collaborated with Cortez to help the tribes which had been oppressed by the Aztecs. Orozco has portrayed Malinche as much more than Cortez' lover.

While Cortez, the civilizer, has the more open face in terms of physical characteristics, he has now taken on the closed dull expression of Malinche. Orozco is always a painter of ambivalence: there is for him no definite answer to the question of the role of the Conquest. This theory is further reinforced by the painting **The Conqueror-Builder and the Indian**

Worker in which Orozco throws into relief the civilising rather than the inhuman side of the Conquest.[28] Whilst an Indian is kneeling and working on blocks of stones, a Spanish master-builder stands holding a set square and a set of plans; he has an expression of determination which is directed towards the building of the new structure. The final depiction of the master-builder with his muscular, voluminous body and head in profile intensifies this impression. Orozco is reaching back here to forms which he used in the mural **Omniciencia** at the Case de los Azulejos.

After the completion of the Murals Orozco was disappointed by the overwhelmingly negative reactions of the Mexican public, although he must have anticipated them particularly as he was aware that both his techniques and use of motifs were still experimental. Orozco's allegorical recourse to Christian iconography after the first paintings was a part of this experiment. He became invoved in a didactical or a strategical exploration into the links between what he wanted to depict and what was intelligible to a Mexican public whose imaginations were still bound to church paintings and the cults of Catholicism. He realised that he had to use this medium to communicate a new sociopolitical and humanistic message whilst the general process of secularisation permeated throughout Mexican society. This ability to use old forms to communicate new messages was introduced to the ENP by Orozco and in this lies the truth of his paintings.

The motifs which occur in the ENP were later used repeatedly by Orozco in murals and easel paintings. So disappointed was he by the reactions of his Mexican compatriots that he went to the USA for six years.

[1]Prior to the National Preparatory School murals Dr Atl (1875-1964), Montenegro (1885-1968) and Xavier Guerrero (1896-1974) had been painting Murals in the colonial building of the former Colegio de San Pedro y San Pablo; these were, however, of little significance for the later mural painting movement. The pictures of Dr Atl were soon overpainted. cf. Jean Charlot, *the Mexican Mural Renaissance*, New Haven/London, 1963, pp.95-106.

[2]cf. José Rojas Garciduenas, *El antiguo Colegio de San Ildefonso*, Mexico 1951.

[3]For a detailed exposition of the development of the murals in the ENP, see Charlot 1963.

[4]José Clemente Orozco, **An Autobiography**, Austin 1962, p.85.

[5]The original frescoes, which today are no longer in existence have also been reproduced in Justino Fernandez, *José Clemente Orozco: Forma e Idea*. Mexico 1942. Illustrations 10-15 (second expanded edition).

[6]The concept as quoted by Charlot 1963, pp.228/229 is quoted in the original Spanish version in *José Clemente Orozco, El artista en Nueva York (cartas a Jean Charlot y textos ineditos, 1925-1929)*, Mexico 1971, pp.133-134. Orozco originally wanted to paint several walls of the courtyard on the ground floor.

[7]The painting **Maternity** could be seen in connection with the theme of **Virginity** from Orozco's early conception if one equates the mother with the Virgin Mary.

[8]cf. Charlot 1963, pp.229-230; the painting which Charlot calls **Spring** has also been called **The Elements** in other literature. cf. Fernandez 1975, p.34 and Antonio Rodriguez, *A History of Mexican Mural Painting*, London 1969, p.188.

[9]In Charlot 1963, p.230 the painting is called **Man Strangling a Gorilla.**

[10]'*Cristo y la bandera roja. Dos simbolos de los universalismos y una puerta que cubre la incognita del futuro.*' Fernandez 1975, p.39. Charlot 1963, p.230 calls the painting **The New Redemption.**

[11]Orozco writes in his autobiography, p.116 '**. . . ladies of the Red or the Green Cross, I don't quite remember which, needed the main patio of the school for a charity bazaar; but instead of politely asking me to suspend my work for a few days, they haughtily ordered me to withdraw, had my scaffolding dismantled on the spot, and hung ornaments for the bazaar directly over the pictures in process. They were loud-voiced in their disapproval and their disgust. In particular the nude figure of a woman with a child displeased them; they believed that it was a Virgin. But I had no intention of painting a virgin, I was painting a mother.**' cf. also Alma Reed on the occurrence, Orozco, New York 1956, p.11.

[12]Anita Brenner, *Idols behind Altars*, New York 1929. (Reprint 1967) p.253. The caricatures of the Catholic women appear in the section entitled **The Reactionaries.**

[13]Also called **Banquet of the Rich**; see Fernandez 1975, p.45 or Rodriguez 1969, p.190.

[14]cf. Orozco's destroyed fresco **Christ Destroying his Cross**.

[15]Rodrigues 1969, p.189.

[16]The Jacobin cap as a symbol of revolution was to recur throughout Orozco's work; it was used many times in the Preparatory School murals.

[17]The illustration of the first version is in Charlot 1963, Fig.37a. Myers 1956, p.92 calls it **Work, Science and Revolution.** The second version '*with its powerful accents of anguish, sorrow and confusion*' is transformed for Myers '*into a more abstract symbol of man's suffering*'. (p.92).

[18]Orozco worked during the revolution as a political caricaturist and also resumed this activity during the Twenties, particularly for the journal of the artists' union *El Machete*. Orozco himself painted scenes similar to these caricatures in 1916 in his brother's restaurant (cf. Charlot 1963, p.129). Schmeckebier writes of the ENP '*The change in Orozco's style from an idealistic symbolism to a factual realism effects a new artistic form that might be called mural caricature*'. Laurence Schmeckebier, *Modern Mexican Art*, Minneapolis 1939 (Reprint 1971), p.55.

[19]In his autobiography. p.116 Orozco writes '**Students in the Preparatory School did not take kindly to the painting. It is safe to say that none of them liked it and they frequently protested to the Secretariat of Education . . .**' The political situation was particularly tense due to the right-orientated military coup by Adolfo de la Huerta in the year 1923.

[20]cf. Charlot 1963, p.285, see also Brenner 1929, p.257.

[21]Orozco began his frescoes in the ENP in July 1923 (cf. Charlot 1963, p.225 and 229) not as early as 1922 as is frequently maintained in error in literature up until the present day. When he had to cease work in 1924, he had just started the painting **The Siege of a Bank** on the second floor which he painted over in 1926. There is no knowledge of photographs of the destroyed frescoes. cf. Charlot 1963, p.235. It is also maintained that he had already painted the Franciscan paintings on the staircases by 1924. cf. Charlot ibid. and Brenner ibid.

[22]The new commission originated mainly as a result of intervention on the part of Alfonso Pruneda: '**Somewhat later still, I returned to the Preparatory School to finish the work I had begun this time under the invaluable protection of Dr· Alfonso Pruneda then rector of the National University**, (Orozco in his autobiography, p.119) cf. also Reed 1956, p.12. As Orozco constantly feared difficulties or a premature interruption he is reputed to have painted the staircase and the second floor at different times in order to prolong the commission. cf. Schmeckebier 1939, pp.66-67.

[23]In the secondary literature the second floor is singled out as being particularly successful because of its formal composition and unity of colour and the way it harmonizes with the architecture. Myers for example writes in 1956, p.93: *The final statement is this building and in many ways the most unified and effective of the murals is the sequence of third floor* (sic) *revolutionary panels.* Schmeckebier in particular draws attention insistently to similarities with the frescoes of the early Italian Renaissance painter Giotto.

[24]The mural **Engineers** was painted by Orozco in the place of a painting carried out by Emilio Garcia Cahero in 1922 on the theme of the Colonial period. Garcia Cahero gave Orozco pernmission to paint over it in 1926.

[25]Orozco in his autobiography: p. 40.

[26]Rodriguez 1969 pp.191-192.

[27]'*La Eva y el Adam paradisiacos surgen recevamente encarnando el simbilico origen de los actuales pueblos americanos*'. Fernandez 1975. pp.41-42.

[28]Brenner 1929. p.264 calls the painting *Alvarado the Conqueror* (Fig.79)

Translation by Jennifer Lanyon

J.C.Orozco

Notes on the Early Frescoes at the National Preparatory School

● In 1916 there was an exhibition of the works that represented my technical progress and my aesthetic ideas up to that time. The latter have not changed in the slightest.

There were then in Mexico only two tendencies in painting: on the one hand, there was a small group bent on exhuming from the Archaeology Museum the decorative motifs of the magnificent art works of the indigenous antiquity, endeavoring to give them all kinds of uses and applications. On the other, there was another group devoted to impressionism and interested only in the skin or the husk of things and even the air that stood between these things and the viewer, but never in things themselves in their intrinsic nature and their density.

This being the artistic atmosphere, the exhibition of which I speak was completely misunderstood by the people, who were unaware of the new tendency represented by the works exhibited, which were called 'caricatures', and, as usual, the people focused their attention only on the theme of the works and even on the author's private life, overlooking the technique employed and the aesthetics of the exhibition.

The archaeological style of seven years ago was replaced by another similar one, which is the prevailing style at present. It consists in attributing to the pure indigene, now in a state of complete degeneration and in the process of disappearing, or pretending to attribute to him, the beautiful objects of the minor folk arts that are the natural product of the creole and the mestizo of the rural areas. It also consists in imposing on the creole and the mestizo of the cities an aesthetic that he neither feels nor can falsify by suppressing and ignoring his own aesthetic facilties. In reality, this conduct is extraordinarily humiliating and will lead to a clash the results of which will be seen in the near future. In some ways, this humiliation is beneficial, because it has served as a reagent to make the humble classes become aware of their powers, shake off their inertia, and awaken.

Painting in its higher forms and painting as a minor folk art differ essentially in this: The former has invariable universal traditions from which no one can separate himself for any reason in any country, and in any epoch. The latter has purely local traditions that vary according to the life, the changes, agitations, and convulsions of each people, each race, each nationality, each social class, and even each family or tribe.

To confuse the one with the other is a serious error, to apply to the one the laws that govern the other is a regrettable mistake because it denaturalizes it and disorients and confuses both of them, causing a delay in their aesthetic development.

That is why one is justified in applying what is understood by 'nationalism' to the minor folk arts. But to try to apply it to great painting, to mural decoration for example, is an inexcusable blunder. Each race will be able to make, and will have to make, its intellectual and emotional contribution to that universal tradition but will *never* be able to impose on it the local and transitory modalities of the minor arts.

Personally, I detest representing in my works the odious and degenerate type of the common people that is generally taken as a 'picturesque' subject to please the tourist or profit at his expense. We are chiefly responsible for having permitted the creation and fostering of the idea that the ridiculous '*charro*' and the vapid '*china poblana*' which represent so-called Mexicanism, and I deeply regret that the no less ridiculous '*jarabe tapatío*' has become popular among the classes who call themselves cultured and educated. The sight of a '*charro*' or '*china*' and the horrendous notes of the '*jarabe*' are inevitably associated with the memory of the nauseating 'Teatro Mexicano', all of which form what are called 'our things'. Whose things? Why do the tritest and most ridiculous attributes of one social class have to belong to a whole country? True nationalism must not consist in this or that theatrical costume or even in this or that popular song of more than doubtful merit, but in our scientific, industrial, or artistic contribution to human civilization. The painter who works in the Italian tradition of the fifteenth and sixteenth centuries is, for example, more of a 'nationalist' than the one who goes crazy over the nationalistic pots and pans that are very suitable for decorating kitchens but not drawing rooms, and even less libraries or laboratories.

These ideas induced me to abjure, once and for all, the painting of '*huaraches*' and dirty cotton pants, and naturally I wish with all my heart that those who use them will discard them and become civilized, but I do not glorify them, just as one does not glorify illiteracy, pulque, or the heaps of trash that 'adorn' our streets.

All aesthetics, of whatever kind, are a movement forward and not backward. In my 1916 exhibition and in all of my serious works there is not a single '*huarache*' or a single '*sombrero*'; the only theme is Humanity and the only tendency is emotion to the maximum, and for this I have

charro: a dandified cowboy in sombrero
    and traditional costume.
china poblana: a woman in the decorative
    local costume of Puebla.
jarabe tapatío: the Mexican hat dance.
huaraches: the rough sandals of the indians.

utilized the REAL AND INTEGRAL representation of
bodies, in themselves and in their relations to one
another.

The real work of art, like a cloud or a tree, has
absolutely nothing to do with morality or
immorality, with good or evil, with wisdom or
ignorance, or with virtue or vice. A mountain
that springs up has nothing of that, and thus must
plastic or musical or literary expression spring
forth, like anything that is born of the impulse of
natural forces and in accordance with their laws.
A painting should not be a commentary but the
fact itself; not a reflection but light itself; not an
interpretation but the thing to be interpreted. It
should not connote any theory or be an anecdote,
story, or history of any kind. It should not contain
opinions about religious, political, or social
matters: absolutely nothing but the plastic fact as
a particular, concrete, and rigorously precise
case. It must not arouse in the viewer any pity or
admiration for the objects, animals, or persons of
the theme. The only emotion it must generate
and transmit must be that which is derived from
the purely plastic, geometric, coldly geometric
phenomenon, organized by a scientific technique.
Everything that is not purely and exclusively the
plastic, geometric language, subjected to the
inescapable laws of mechanics, expressible by an
equation, is a subterfuge to conceal impotence; it
is literature, politics, philosophy, whatever you
will, but it is not painting. When an art loses its
purity and is denaturalized, it degenerates,
becomes abominable, and finally disappears.

1923

Return to the Battlefield, fresco, 1926
Preparatory School

J.C.Orozco

Unpublished notes
Probably written for the journal, *La Falange*

● **Triumph.**

Everyone triumphs or can triumph because
there is always an audience that applauds or
acclaims every talent, and every imbecile, and
every scoundrel.

The only ones who fail are those who do not
know how to find their audience, or cannot.

Verses.

Some poems have very good spelling and a
magnificent polish but are not worth a peanut.
Some paintings boast the golden proportion and
that famous cubist technique. They are not worth
a peanut either.

Painting THAT IS NOT UNDERSTOOD is pseudo-
cubist painting, that is, painting done with so-
called scientific FORMULAS, imported from
Paris. Such 'painting' is not understood by
anyone, not even the one who does it.

Art is, above all, GRACE. Where there is no
GRACE there is no Art. GRACE is not achieved by
so-called cubist formulas.

As fishermen reap much gain from troubled
waters, so too HACK PAINTERS derive great profit
from confusion.

Be wary of painting that needs explanations in
order to be 'understood'. What would you think if,
while you were enjoying some good music, an
erudite musicologist started to give an
'explanatory' lecture?

There are also SCHOLARS of painting: they know
SO MUCH about it that through their works pass the
paintings of all the others . . . except their own!

Painting for the People? But the People do
their own painting: they don't need anyone to do
it for them.

Painting is not HEARD, IT IS SEEN and in order
TO SEE IT one merely has TO HAVE EYES. Pay no
attention to what others say: judge for yourself
with YOUR OWN EYES.

It is a lie that 'one has to be a connoisseur' in
order to understand and feel a painting; the
roughest and most ignorant man can be attracted
and subjugated by beauty, wherever it may be
found. It would be a fine state of affairs if we had
to be 'connoisseurs' of the art of cooking in order
to be able to enjoy a good meal!

1923

Both these texts were unpublished during Orozco's lifetime. They were
previously published in English in: J. C. Orozco **The Artist in New York:
Letters to Jean Charlot and unpublished writings, 1925-1929,** Austin,
University of Texas Press, 1974. Translated by Ruth L.C.Simms.

Las Soldaderas (The Camp Followers), oil on canvas, 1926 (cat. 32)

Left:
Revolutionary Trinity,
Preparatory School fresco
1926

Omniscience, 1925:
Mural in the Casa de los Azulejos
(now a department store)
Mexico City

Total area 46 sq. metres

Social Revolution, 1926:
Mural in the Escuela Industrial
(now the Workers' Educational Centre),
Orizaba, Veracruz, Mexico

Total area 46.6 sq. metres

In its classically derived subject matter and theme centred on an allegory of *The Creation*, this mural looks back to Orozco's first attempts at the National Preparatory School.

Above workers with spades and rifles start to build a new life out of the carnage of the Revolution. Below on either side of the window are the bereaved, huddled women — an intimation of the tragedy of war. This mural was completed early in 1926 before Orozco returned to Mexico City to work in similar vein on the National Preparatory School.

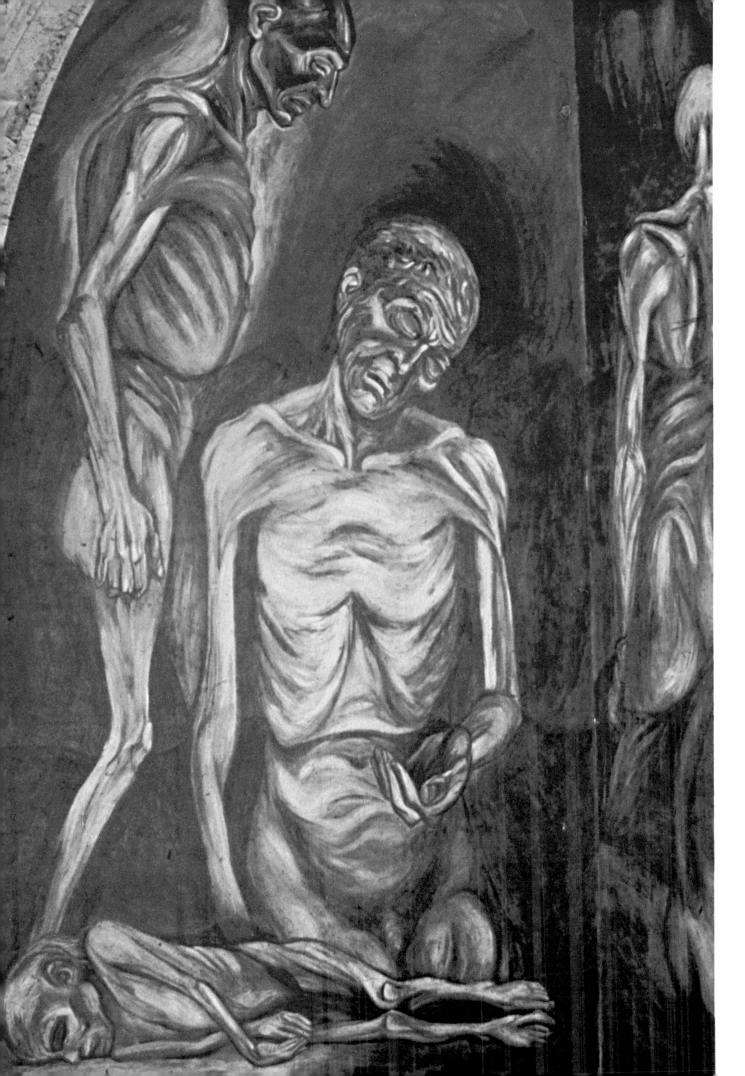

Previous pages: left, **The Victims** 1936; fresco side panel to
The People and its False Leaders in the Assembly Hall, University of Guadalajara, Mexico.
Top Right, **Creative Man**: the cupola.
Bottom Right, **The People and its False Leaders**; the wall panels.
These two murals comprise the University of Guadalajara cycle.

J.C.Orozco: Extracts from a letter to Jean Charlot from New York, 23 February 1928

Very dear Jean:
I have just received your letter. The Art Center show—a total, absolute, and definite failure: FACTS: the gallery is bad, just amateurs and beginners, the room dark, the director an imbecile, complete chaos, after one week there wasn't even a catalog. They shuffled the pictures, and as those by Pacheco, Ruiz, and Montenegro were the largest ones, they put them in the best places, those that were most visible. There were also Hidalgo's little wax monkeys and dressed fleas. The very few people who came just laughed and joked or felt /'disappointed.'/ The serious art press, like *The Arts, Art News,* etc., didn't say a word, neither did the critics ... Pach himself assures me that the director is a scoundrel, that he is just there to earn ten thousand dollars a year. As to that Mrs. Paine, they say she is a kind of Dr Atl in skirts, involved in a thousand different schemes, all half-baked and very different from one another; and there is no denying that she deceived everyone in Mexico.

As to the 'Friends' (?) I had here, I've sent them all to the devil, because they treated me with scorn and humiliated me. I am completely isolated, but happily I don't need 'protectors', 'guardians', /'managers',/ 'critics', papas', 'prodders', or 'helpers', they are all a flock of false and self-seeking persons who only see one as an object to be exploited.

PAINTING: Have I seen painting! An extraordinary exhibition of Spanish painting: EL GRECO, GOYA, VELÁZQUEZ, etc., pictures lent by millionaire collectors, at the Metropolitan Museum. 67 pictures, 13 of which are Grecos, how can I put into words the impression they made on me? The moderns may be 'great men' or 'great masters', but El Greco is a God. What can I say about Goya? I had a certain prejudice against Velázquez, but in the presence of the evidence one has to capitulate: if to paint is to put colors on a surface, only his equals can do it with the same mastery and perfection. . . .

Several days ago there was also another very important show: 24 Cézannes, half of them pictures lent by private individuals and half from Rosenberg. I went every morning for a week to study Cézanne. Perhaps very close to El Greco. Good old Matisse disappears.

An /exhibit/ of many Degas. I am not enthusiastic.

An /exhibit/ of many Giorgio de Chiricos at the **Valentine Gallery,**/camouflage, trick,/ extravagance, and farce, in short: very 'daring'(?) but *nothing.* That Valentine Gallery belongs to Dudensing and Matisse's son, very nice fellows,

The Requiem, lithograph, 1928

you'll get to know them, their gallery is very pretty, Covarrubias is going to have another /exhibit/ there soon. They say that Chirico sold a lot.

Forain: he is really pretty bad.

LITHOGRAPHY: I am going to do it, it's easy, it doesn't have to be done on stone, there are some special plates, I already have two of them. There is a Mr Miller who has a lithography studio here and he is the one who makes the prints for the art galleries. The plates I bought (26 × 43 centimeters) cost 50 cents each, the printing of the first 12 proofs costs 10 dollars, and each additional one is 25 cents, plus the paper. It's expensive for me, but I'll see if I can manage it.

Diegoff Riveritch Romanoff: Still a big threat to us. As I told your mother when I answered her letter, the idea that we are all his disciples is very well entrenched here. To talk about 'Indians', 'revolution', 'Mexican renaissance', 'folk arts', '*retablos*', etc., etc., is to talk about Rivera. . . .

The /Mexican fashion/ or *mode de Mexique,* whatever you want to call it, that farce, is now passing. One proof of this is the exhibition of Diegoff's work that was held at the so-called Wheye or Whye Gallery. It is not a gallery at all, just a very small book-store, like 'Cultura' or Robredo's, a kind of Volador in miniature, because it has a little of everything, even nicknacks. And during the winter they have continuous shows, each lasting for 3 days, you can imagine what they are like. One of them was Diegoff's and that was where I saw his cubist jokes for the first time, there was one with a toothbrush glued to the canvas and a picture in the style of Zuloaga and watercolors in the style of Cézanne, etc. Of course the press spoke very well of it and mentioned the Mexican Renaissance and

42

the Indians and the Revolution and called him /'many-sided'/ and /'great man'./ A Renaissance with toothbrushes!!!!....

Tell me Juan: aren't you angry about anything I've said in this letter? Are you still my friend?

Thanks for your article and I am looking forward to reading it. Write me at the new address because I plan to move, my room is so small that I can't work.

Your friend, CLEMENTE

Words between obliques were written by Orozco in English
Translation by Ruth L.C.Simms

Los Muertos (The Dead),
oil on canvas, 1931
(cat. 58)

New World, New Races and New Art
by José Clemente Orozco

First published in 'Creative Art'. Magazine of
Fine and Applied Art (N.Y.). January, 1929. Vol. 4, No. 1.

● The art of the New World cannot take root in the old traditions of the Old World nor in the aboriginal traditions represented by the remains of our ancient indian peoples. Although the art of all races and of all times has a common value — human, universal — each new cycle must work for itself, must create, must yield its own production, its individual share to the common good.

To go solicitously to Europe, bent on poking about its ruins in order to import them and servilely to copy them, is no greater error than is the looting of the indigenous remains of the New World with the object of copying, with equal servility, its ruins or its present folk-lore. However picturesque and interesting these may be, however productive and useful ethnology may find them, they cannot furnish a point of departure for the new creation. To lean upon the art of the aborigines, whether it be of antiquity or of the present day, is a sure indication of impotence and of cowardice, in fact, of fraud.

If NEW races have appeared upon the lands of the NEW WORLD, in a new spiritual and physical medium. Any other road is plain cowardice.

Already, the architecture of Manhattan is a new value, something that has nothing to do with Egyptian pyramids, with the Paris Opera, with the Giralda of Seville, or with Saint Sofia, any more than it has to do with the maya palaces of Chichen-Itza or with the 'pueblos' of Arizona.

Imagine the New York Stock Exchange in a french cathedral. Imagine the brokers all rigged out like indian chieftains, with head feathers or with mexican sombreros. The architecture of Manhattan is the first step. Painting and sculpture must certainly follow as inevitable second steps.

The highest, the most logical, the purest and strongest form of painting is the mural. In this form alone, is it one with the other arts — with all the others.

It is, too, the most disinterested form, for it cannot be made a matter of private gain; it cannot be hidden away for the benefit of a certain privileged few.

It is for the people. It is for ALL.

1929

Prometheus:
Mural in Pomona College, Claremont, California
1930

Total area 70 sq. metres

Top: **Prometheus**
Bottom left: Side panel, **Zeus, Hera and Io**
Bottom right: Side panel, **Agitated Centaurs**

General view of Frary Hall,
Pomona College

Parade of Zapatistas,
oil and tempera on canvas, 1931
(cat. 55)

The building of the New School had
just been completed and the room which
housed these murals was at that time
a cafeteria

The New School for Social Research, New York, 1930

Total area 81 sq. metres

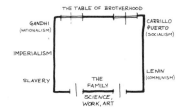

Top: **The Family (Return of the Worker)**
Bottom: **Science, Work, Art (Allegory of Arts and Sciences)**

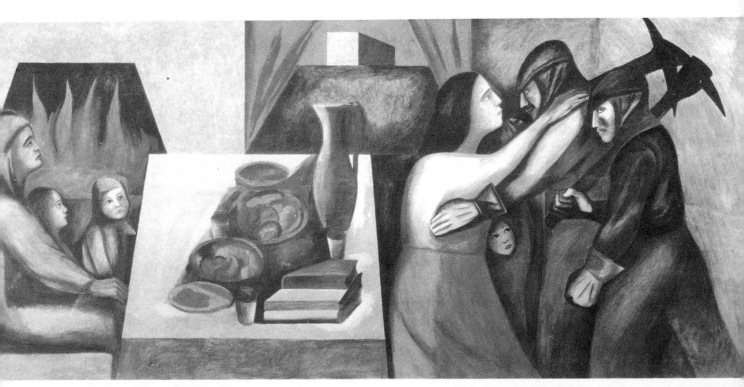

Top: **Carrillo Puerto and Lenin**
Middle: **The Table of Brotherhood**
Bottom: **Gandhi, Imperialism, Slavery**

Laurance P. Hurlburt
Notes on Orozco's North American Murals: 1930 - 34

In terms of theme, composition, and expression the three murals Orozco painted in the United States during the early 1930s played a key role in his artistic development, and paved the way for the series of monumental expressionistic works of art he created in Mexico during the late 1930s and early 1940s. Although limited by space and far from completed with research, I can nonetheless bring to light new evidence of various aspects of this important period in Orozco's career, particularly matters concerning the patronage of the murals.[1]

Orozco's first North American mural commission, at Pomona College (Claremont, California) did not materialize until more than two years after his arrival in the United States.[2] The mural owes its existence to the enthusiasm and unorthodox actions of José Pijoan, a Catalonian who was then adjunct (i.e. non-tenured) professor of Spanish civilization at the College, and to the interest of Sumner Spaulding, architect of Frary Hall which had been dedicated in 1929. Spaulding proposed a mural for the arched recess in the southern end (35 by 18 feet; the speaker's rostrum) in the refectory, which was designed in the Spanish Romanesque idiom, in early March 1930.[3] In an unusual but typically impetuous move, Pijoan, appealed directly to the students for contributions for Orozco's fee, set at $2000, and they pledged half of the amount, with Pijoan to raise the other half by himself.[4] Students from this time recall that they were successful in raising approximately $600 and in late May George Marston, a trustee of the College who had donated the funds for Frary Hall, personally gave $1000 for the mural, stipulating that *At the present there should be no commitment for the decoration of the four walls* [i.e. of Frary Hall] *and I myself would be willing to limit the painting to the wall where a beginning has been made, until we can judge more properly of the style and effect of the painting.*[5] Orozco arrived at Claremont with his friend and fellow artist Juan Jorge Crespo de la Serna, who would assist him, on 22 March. Orozco was dismayed, according to Alma Reed, to find out for the first time that an adequate mural fund did not exist.[6]

The Promethean theme was, according to Robert C. Denison, member of the College philosophy department, one of three suggested by Pijoan, and the one favoured by Orozco.[7] Not only is the theme of Prometheus bringing fire, symbolizing knowledge, to mankind entirely appropriate for a college hall, but Orozco strongly identified with his particular interpretation of the theme — the sacrifice of the creative rebel for the benefit of mankind, whose responses to his act vary from rejection, apathy, ignorance, and acceptance. Indeed, this theme of the rebel and the masses would be the central concern of Orozco's later work, most stunningly treated in the

Guadalajara series of 1936-39. Orozco had been exposed to classical Greek themes, and particularly the Promethean myth, during his association with the Alma Reed-Eva Sikelianos circle in New York, deeply committed to ideals such as Greek culture and Indian independence.[8] Also, the Prometheus image was very much in the air locally, having been included in the prize-winning design of Erwin Hetsch in the 1929 world wide competition for a mural hall at the Los Angeles Museum of History and Art. The theme decided, Orozco, according to Pijoan, *retreated three days in his silent way and produced a sketch of the work as it is now. I was exceedingly surprised. I could not help admiring the great originality of this old subject.*[9] At this point Sumner Spaulding appears to have entered the standoff between Pijoan and the administration, and made the key decision for going ahead with the mural:

When Orozco's charcoal sketch was shown to a committee of trustees and faculty, they could make nothing of it. They put the decision up to Sumner Spaulding, architect of the magnificent hall. Spaulding had never heard of Orozco. He took the sketch into a cloister and found himself thinking of Michelangelo. That decided him. The fresco was painted.[10]

Inside Frary Hall one first reacts to Orozco's **Prometheus** as a superb piece of architectural decoration, the fitting climax to the progression of the great Gothic arches down the hall. The enormous Titan, bent on one knee and the other leg askew, is in the act of taking fire from the heavens. Pijoan, the initiator of the project, supplies a contemporary reaction to the work:

Our Prometheus is not like the ancient floorwalker easily handling a torch. He is on the contrary the great man, victim of his own deeds. Mankind around him tries to receive a spark from the flame, not to use on the anvil to make weapons and tools but to warm of the fire their cold souls and change from frozen ghosts to real living beings. In the fresco of Orozco the flame produces a variety of effects on the mortals about to receive it. Some embrace each other; some stab each other; some preach; some flee.[11]

Orozco himself stressed that the two important matters in the painting were **'Prometheus and the crowd'**; on the crowd: **'the crowd is just a crowd, like you see anywhere. The crowds are always in motion — I have tried to make them dynamic. They move; they do things.'** The figures on the side panels — to the left Zeus, Hera, and Io; to the right agitated centaurs — are of lesser interest and represent **'the ancient times that Prometheus is upsetting by giving knowledge to mankind. They are only a part of the universal mythology.'**[12] The place of the **Prometheus** mural in Orozco's career — its relationship to his classical artistic education, and to the romantic-symbolist and expressionist movements of the early 20th century in Mexico, to Orozco's murals of the

51

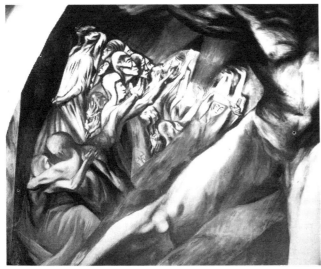

Prometheus, 1930
two details of the crowd

1920s and his innovative 'direct expression' in this mural — are beyond the scope of this paper, and at any rate, have been discussed in an excellent article by David Scott.[13]

The opposition to Orozco's artistic presence in Claremont, a conservative community of orange growers and strong religious sentiments (Pomona College was founded by the Congregationalist Church), continued for a time after the mural's completion. Yet, besides the protests of the misinformed (who for example, complained of Orozco's 'communistic' politics) one sector of the population, including members of the College, felt that the mural simply was artistically inappropriate to the ideals of Western civilization which, stemming from Greece and Rome, were represented contemporarily by Pomona College. These people strongly objected to Orozco's expressionistic modernism — the distortions of the human figure for example — and felt that his entire approach was offensive, a violation of classical canons of beauty (or 'monstrous disfiguration', in their terms). The irony here is that so-called Indian and/or Mexican pagan distortions objected to derived from European Expressionsism.[14]

During the painting of **Prometheus**, Pijoan conceived of a grand plan for decorating the entire interior of Frary Hall as a '*Hall of Giants*', which would have depicted battles between the Titans and Gods on the side walls, and facing the Prometheus, '*the great Titanomachia or the destruction of the Titans by Jupiter's thunderbolts.*'[15] However, there was little chance that this series could have been painted, although it apparently terrified the Administration, as Pijoan had already resigned in April 1930.[16] By 1 May 1930, Orozco had already completed arrangements for painting murals at the New School for Social Research in New York.

Orozco's New School murals clearly represent the least important of his North American work. This can be accounted for by several factors, including the nature of the commission. Dr Alvin Johnson's acceptance of '*your* [Orozco's] *generous offer through your agent, Mrs Alma Reed, to honor our new building with your work,*'[17] indicates that it was to be a non-paying commission. Alma Reed, in a letter to Johnson, President of the New School, completely details the matter of the New School commission:

It is his wish and my own . . . that the matter remain in its present status, which affords me the great honor of remaining the donor of the mural, outside the payment of the amount so kindly contributed by you towards his studio during the progress of the work and his railroad fare from San Francisco.

And it is only right and proper that this cheerfully assumed (though at the time very difficult) responsibility of making it possible for Sr. Orozco to meet his personal and his family needs during the progress of this work at the New School remains my own, since the whole idea of the frescoes for the New School originated in my own mind; because the work itself represents profoundly my own point of view and idealism, and because with the Mexican panel, my name will associated in Mexican history.[18]

Orozco himself referred to the close personal involvement of Alma Reed to the paintings, when he said to her on the day the murals were to be dedicated (19 January 1931): '**You are always going to feel very much at home here, Almita. You will be among your friends; it is just another Ashram.**'[19]

Indeed, the imagery of the New School panels, painted during a period of 46½ days in the cramped quarters of the low-ceiling cafeteria (forty feet square; the paintings are six feet high), depends heavily on themes closely associated with the 'Ashram'. Above all, in the group's general altruistic spirit — in Reed's term, 'the common goal of brotherhood,' the paintings derive from Orozco's involvement with the group. Thus, the **Table of Brotherhood**, a peaceful gathering of the various races of the world, portrays specific members of the 'Ashram'.[20] The west wall depicts two aspects of the international struggle for peace and brotherhood, **Socialism** (Yucatán) and **Communism** (the Soviet Union); the painting of Felipe Carrillo Puerto, framed by the 'Castillo' of Chichén-Itza and the peasant 'Leagues of Resistance' (i.e., against the henequen planters) he established, held close personal meaning for Reed.[21] Similarly the east wall, **Nationalism**, picturing Gandhi's struggle against British imperialism, held strong meaning for the 'Ashram', where Sarojini Naidu, a poetess and fellow worker of Gandhi's, at this time raising aid for the Indian movement, often appeared. In **The Slaves** section of this wall we encounter one of the few places in the mural where the imagery and point of view are typically those of Orozco, and this painting anticipates his portrayal of the suffering masses in Guadalajara (University, Government Palace). **The Family (Return of the Worker)**, facing **Table of Brotherhood**, completes the paintings inside the room (where classes are now held), and presents the benefits of revolution and brotherhood: the worker returning to his family and enjoying employment, housing, warmth, and food. Outside this room **Allegory of Arts and Sciences** represents man as scientist, worker, and artist, a theme which would be expanded many times in size and conception in the University of Guadalajara cupola.

Orozco in front of
Allegory of Arts and Sciences, October 1945

If the nature of the commission placed thematic constraints on Orozco, resulting in a portrayal of contemporary doctrinaire socialism and an uncharacteristically positive view of the human condition, Orozco himself imposed an arbitrary compositional scheme, Jay Hambidge's theories of 'Dynamic Symmetry', on his paintings at the New School. Orozco devotes several pages to Hambidge's ideas, which enjoyed popularity at this time and whose quasi-scientific basis must have appealed to Orozco, with his background in mathematics and engineering, in his **Autobiography,** and I include the most pertinent passages:

'This painting is of a special nature in being based upon the geometric-aesthetic principles of the investigator Jay Hambidge. Apart from purely personal motives of expression, I wanted to discover how convincing and useful those principles were and what their possibility was . . .

Hambidge himself carried his conclusions too far, but he did the arts a service in providing them with an instrument without which they cannot survive, a very old but forgotten instrument: geometry . . .

After doing the pictures at the New School I abandoned the overrigorous and scientific methods of Dynamic Symmetry, but I kept what was fundamental and inevitable and with this I shaped new ways of working. I had the explanation of many former errors and I saw new roads opening up.' [22]

Hambidge maintained that two types of 'symmetry' (or design) existed in all works of art: the 'static', arithmetical subdivision of forms, and the 'dynamic', geometrical subdivision of form — the basis here being the use of the square and its diagonal to form 'root rectangles' (i.e., rectangles formed by a square and its diagonals where the relationship between the longer and shorter side is 1: 0.618 — the classical 'Golden Section'). Hambidge believed that 'Dynamic Symmetry' existed in nature, man, and the highest forms of art; in his view, Egyptian and classical Greek art.[23] Although 'Dynamic Symmetry' formed the basis for Orozco's composition at Pomona College, he did not paint **Prometheus** in strict reliance to Hambidge's system, whereas the New School paintings slavishly follow the dictums of 'dynamic Symmetry'. The drawings emerge primarily as geometric designs, and the paintings can easily be analyzed as arrangements of various 'root' and 'whirling square' rectangles.

Various factors, then — patronage of a friend who served as his dealer, a conscious submission to the dictates of 'Dynamic Symmetry', a small, cramped architectural environment, perhaps the pressure of painting murals for the first time in the nation's art centre, New York — contributed to the weakness, certainly in comparison to Pomona College and Dartmouth, of the New School murals.[24] Fundamentally one misses the fiercely independent spirit characteristic of Orozco — as Octavio Paz says, '*He was a truly free man and artist and, something extraordinary for Mexico, he was not afraid to exercise his freedom*' [25] — which is so harnessed at the New School. Yet, I would argue that the work represented an important learning experience for Orozco, particularly in terms of his immersion in 'Dynamic Symmetry'. If the unfortunate immediate result, an overly rigid, sterile composition, must be considered a failure, Hambidge's system would provide Orozco with a most important instrument, which he would first employ at Dartmouth: a geometric framework for his essentially spontaneous painting style.

Contrary to the impression created by Reed, Dartmouth College officials actively sought out Orozco to paint murals at Dartmouth, and were interested in him long before his work at the New School.[26] Further, Reed maintains that 'two years at Dartmouth on the modest salary of a visiting lecturer had provided the painter with only a bare living', which is simply not true. In fact, between May 1932 and February 1934 Orozco, as visiting artist, was paid $7700 wages and received $2177.05 for painting materials and expenses, placing him in the upper 20 per cent of faculty salaries during the academic year 1933-34.[27] At this time this represented *much* more than a 'bare living'!

Orozco first came to Dartmouth on 2 May 1932 to paint a demonstration fresco, **Man Released from the Mechanistic** (7 by 8 feet) above the door connecting the art building, Carpenter Hall, and Baker Library. The favourable response to Orozco's work, plus Orozco's own enthusiasm about the vast expanse of the then undecorated Reserve room, the bottom level of the recently constructed Baker library (3000 square feet; a long hall c.150 feet long and 26 feet wide) resulted in the far larger Dartmouth commission:

However, on his own initiative, and entirely without request from us, Orozco figured out exactly the amount of wall space that he had desired was available in this room,

and that this was broken by the basement windows into panels of exactly the size that he had in mind for the development of this subject. Thereupon he presented to us the formal proposal that in this location which the usual artist would not be interested in and on these walls which had been entirely without decoration he should be allowed to develop his major theme, the desireable space for which he had long sought. Moreover, he argued, and our authorities in archaeology, in anthropological sociology, and in art bore him out, that at Dartmouth more than anyplace in the country the theme was appropriate in view of our original relationship to the Indian culture of the country, despite the fact that our relationship was one of trying to overthrow it. Orozco's ultra-enthusiasm in regard to the whole project seemed to be based on a conviction that at Dartmouth more than anywhere else in the world the circumstances existed which would make his work of major appropriateness.' [28]

Total area
277 sq. metres

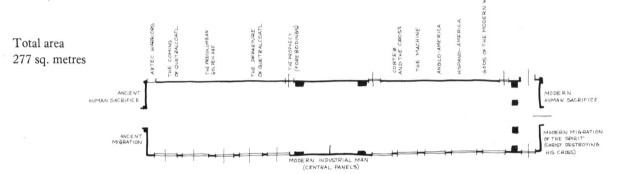

Top: Plan of the Dartmouth College Murals
Middle and bottom: General views of the West and East walls

The Dartmouth paintings, the culminating work of the North American period, are Orozco's personal interpretation, in epic narrative terms, of the evolution of civilization in America, and a commentary of its present state. At Baker Library Orozco liberated his composition from the confines of 'Dynamic Symmetry', employing only a general geometric armature, a 'geometric skeleton', on which he painted directly. Then, here Orozco more effectively coordinated the relationship between that of the daily work patches (*giornate*) and the composition, in many places painted over two adjoining sections in *fresco secco* to create a heightened sense of surface unity. The Dartmouth paintings, specifically the **Ancient Migration** panel and all the post-Cortesian panels, are marked by a much more bold and loose handling of the brushwork — which has the effect of more effectively carrying the image to the spectator over the great distance involved — the first appearance of a tendency which will be increased during the 1936-39 Guadalajara paintings, when the pigments are at times splattered on the walls.[29] Finally, at Dartmouth the paintings are devoid of thematic influences derived from the 'Ashram', and the socio-political pessimism of these works points the way to the similarly increased tendency towards the negative political view expressed in the 1936-39 murals.

Orozco intended his treatment of an 'American idea', to use his term, as a comprehensive ideological vision of civilization on this continent:

'The American continental races are now becoming aware of their own personality as it emerges from the two cultural currents, the indigenous and the European. The great American myth of Quetzalcoatl is a living one, embracing both elements and pointing clearly by its prophetic nature, to the responsibility shared equally by the two Americas of creating here an authentic American civilization.' [30]

He depicted the turgid beginnings of American civilization — wandering and barbarity — in **Ancient Migration** and **Ancient Human Sacrifice.** Note photos of the work-in-progress, which reveal that Orozco actually began with the last painting, chronologically, in the Quetzalcoatl series, the **Prophecy**, and that the first full panel to be painted was **Sacrifice**, followed by the Quetzalcoatl series. The first painting, chronologically, in Orozco's sequence, **Migration**, because of its looser brushstroke, identical to that in the post-Cortesian paintings, was thus painted last. The next group of five paintings (two smaller works flanking three large ones of c.10 by 13 feet), a superb example of Orozco's ability of plastic integration, depict the legend of Quetzalcoatl, the primary figure in pre-Cortesian indigenous thought.[31] In the first of these Quetzalcoatl rises, a benevolent, creative force of energy, dispells the heretofore dominant evil gods, and awakens mankind, and culture results. Next, Orozco celebrates the positive achievements of the native pre-Cortesian civilizations,

made possible by Quetzalcoatl's gift: agriculture, art, and astronomy. Lastly, Quetzalcoatl wrathfully departs on a raft of snakes, rejected by the people that benefited so greatly from his benign presence. In these panels Orozco succeeded wonderfully in his conscious intent to create an integrated relationship of plastic form and colour:

'Orozco says he wishes to convey the feeling of a morning and an evening in these Quetzalcoatl panels, the rising and setting of the sun. And it is easy to see that the plastic forms and the colors have been selected to express that sort of feeling; the brilliant array of many colored gods in confident hieratic postures about the dynamic figure of the Life-Giver, on the one hand, and on the other, the lone stooping figure surrounded only by the sombre tones of a stormy sea and the sinister black menace of writhing serpents.' [32]

Above, below and overleaf: Work in progress at Dartmouth showing the order in which the panels were painted

The ominous tone of Quetzalcoatl's departure is fully justified in the discordant, jarring imagery of the five post-Cortesian paintings, in which Orozco portrayed the complete change he saw in American civilization after the Spanish Conquest.[33] European civilization and technology is represented by the looming figure of Cortez, his military efforts supported by the Church and his indomitable will illustrated by the flaming ships in the background, which he had burnt to forstall his troops' talk of leaving Mexico. Orozco provides a sense of ideological linkage between the effect of Cortez's arrival and our own 20th-century industrial civilization, an impersonal scene of abstract mechanized shapes and forms:

'. . . to the triumphant militarism of the early period of exploitation he ties the triumphant mechanism of the later period: the two are graphically connected — as they were in history — by the prostrate figures of Cortes' captives, who are represented as being fed into the maw of the machine, their arms twisting into stumps as they are gripped by the steel.' [34]

Next Orozco contrasts Anglo and Hispanic society: the strong sense of order and efficiency which has produced regimentation and ultimately dullness in the scene of the New England 'schoolmarm' and her humanoid students is juxtaposed with its antithesis, the chaos and destruction Orozco saw at work in Hispano-American society. In the last painting of the long east wall, **Gods of the Modern World**, Orozco denounces what he believed to be the sterility and meaninglessness of modern institutional education, a grotesque scene in which a skeleton, prone on a bed of books, has given birth to a dead foetus, watched over by cadavers in academic garb.[35] The Western civilizational cycle ends as **Modern Human Sacrifice** and **Modern Migration of the Spirit** face their earlier counterparts in the west end of the building at a distance of 150 feet. The **Sacrifice**, a weak cartoony treatment of the futility of war and nationalistic 'Unknown Soldier' ceremonies, fares poorly in comparison with **Migration**, the magnificent climax of the post-Cortesian panels. Here a Pantocrator-type Christ militantly destroys his Cross, while in the background rises a mountainous junk heap of various remnants of modern civilization. Orozco, in this 'Creator-Destroyer' figure — as contrasted to the positive creative force symbolized by Quetzalcoatl in the indigenous American civilization series — seems to be calling for the total destruction of the prevailing forms of modern politics, religion, and culture. The Baker Library murals themselves end ambiguously with a set of small paintings, **Modern Industrial Man**[36] opposite the delivery desk in the Reserve room area and separate from the west and east wings. The paintings are thus architecturally removed from the flow of the western civilization epic, and they bear little relationship to the imagery and predominantly negative tone of the post-Cortesian panels, nor to Orozco's subsequent treatment of the workers or masses theme.

Orozco emerged from the North American murals as a fully mature artist, and would proceed to create an astonishing cycle of expressionistic masterworks on Mexican walls during the next several years. Perhaps it is most appropriate to end my consideration of this vital period of Orozco's career with an excerpt from an unpublished letter (from a person wishing to learn mural painting from Orozco), in which Orozco speaks not only about conditions at Dartmouth, but also concerning devotion to the art of mural painting:

'The mural I have been painting here in the College is a work done under special and unusual circumstances. It has to be finished in the shortest possible time, and for that reason it is not possible to have apprentices of any kind. All my effort and attention have to be concentrated on the mural.

There has been much misunderstanding among the public and art students about fresco painting. As a medium it is simple and easier than any other used by artists and it can be learned by any student in just ten minutes, and then by personal research and experiment it is possible to get some skill to use it effectively. Now, the mural conception and technique is quite another matter that requires a life-long study of the most complex problems, no matter what the medium used for painting.' [37]

[1] I am at present in California conducting research on a project involving the activities of Orozco, Rivera, and Siqueiros in the United States during the 1930s and their influence on North American artists, funded by the National Endowment for the Humanities.
[2] In characteristically laconic fashion, Orozco wrote in his **Autobiography** (University of Texas Press, 1962, p.123) that **'there was little to hold me in Mexico in 1927, and I resolved to go to New York . . .'** Among the factors involved here: the control of important public mural commissions by Diego Rivera in the mid and late 1920s. Siqueiros also fared badly with commissions during this period, and in fact abandoned art for union organizing activities in western Mexico during 1925-30. For Orozco's difficult years in New York, 1927-29, see his letters to Jean Charlot, published as **The Artist in New York** (University of Texas, 1971).

[3] Pomona and Scripps Colleges newspaper, *Student Life*, 6 March, 1930.
[4] *Student Life*, 19 March, 1930; Pijoan also mentions the $2000 figure in a letter appearing in the special 'Fresco Edition' of 19 April.
[5] a. Letters of Bob Brown (Class of 1933 and Freshman President) and Glen Turner to Dean Sheldon Beatty; October and November 1957 (from President's papers, Pomona College).
b. Marston statement in letter to Pijoan from President Edmunds dated 27 May, 1930 (Pomona College President's files).
[6] a. For Alma Reed's account of this period, see her biography *Orozco* (Oxford University Press, 1956, pp.169-188). She maintains (p.171) that *'The sum mentioned to use available for the mural was five thousand dollars, and we were given to understand that the money was already on hand or had been guaranteed.'* This figure appears *nowhere* in articles published at this time, nor in official college memos, letters on file, or published

communication between Orozco, Pijoan, and Crespo (published in *Orozco*, by Luis Cardoza y Aragón, UNAM, Mexico, 1959). To further complicate matters, Reed (p.186) asserts that President Edmunds, in ceremonies honouring the artist and the mural in mid-June, presented Orozco with a check for 'less than half the originally stipulated five thousand dollars'. Yet there is no record of any such payment in College files; moreover, Earl and Dorothy Merritt, friends of Orozco during his stay in Claremont, say that Orozco told them that he had received *no* money for his work, and, finally, in his *Autobiography* (p.139) Orozco writes: **'Still the work got done, and I went back to San Francisco — though with less money than when I arrived the first time, in 1917. It was not even enough to pay for my return passage to New York.'**
b. The College, however, did provide for the artists' room and board; Pomona College memo

dated 15 April, 1949 (a conversation with George Sumner, College Controller in 1930) and interview with Thomas Beggs, head of Pomona College art department in 1930, 5 March, 1980.

[7] *Student Life*, 7 September 1932, 'Interview with Dr. Denison', a supporter of the mural. Other possible themes were 'The Last Judgment' and 'Founders of North American Educational Institutions'.

[8] From accounts of the activities of the Reed-Sikelianos salon, the 'Ashram', and their involvement of a production of *Prometheus Bound* see Reed, pp.173-75. Orozco's **Autobiography** (pp.127-35) includes his 'rebaptism' as Panselenos, the Byzantine mural painter.

[9] a. Pijoan letter to *Student Life*, 23 March 1937.
b. Yet Pijoan showed another, earlier, version of the mural study to Thomas Beggs, who recalls (interview of 5 March 1980):

'... it was a figure dashing horizontally, the body was a horizontal line with the leg extended and one leg supporting him, and the arm outstretched, so that arm and leg and extended torch made a horizontal line that repeated the horizontal of the wainscotting. But I suggested that, perhaps instead of using just the horizontal line, if it would hit the fall of the arch, that if it were tilted up, it would support the arch.'

I have not as yet located this drawing, and another drawing similar to the completed painting, possibly that mentioned by Pijoan, reproduced in *Student Life*, 4 November 1930.

[10] This account by the art critic, Arthur Millier, in the *Los Angeles Times*, 4 February 1951.

[11] a. Pijoan letter to *Los Angeles Times*, 8 August 1930.
b. The mural was painted on 'Acosticon' (plaster board containing a good deal of cotton; used to prevent echoes), and Orozco applied the final, or intonaco, coat directly to this, **'without much hope of a good adherence.'** He was pleasantly surprised to find in 1946 that the painting remained **'apparently in excellent condition'**

(from *Textos de Orozco*, Mexico 1955, p.79).
c. Jean Ames, artist and member of Scripps College art faculty, watched Orozco paint and recalls that he worked in a spontaneous, improvisational manner directly on the wall from a large sketch of the entire mural held by a young Mexican boy. He used a student grade water-colour mixing tray, mixing very small amounts of pigment at one time, and student quality brushes (approximately no. 12 camel hair). Further, Orozco was bothered by the unfamiliar Canadian lime he had to use, and worried that, if not properly slaked, it would burn out the pigment colors (interview 12 August 1980).

[12] *Student Life*, 17 May 1930, 'Orozco on his fresco'.

[13] See David Scott 'Orozco's Prometheus: Summation, Transition, Innovation', in *College Art Journal*, Fall 1955, to my mind the pioneering post-1930s work on 20th-century Mexican muralism.

[14] An example was David Scott's father, a member of the Pomona College Speech Department at the time, with a PhD in philosophy and background as minister, and a solid grounding in the classics. Professor Scott's distaste for what the mural represented — that is, what he saw as the abandonment of the ideals of western culture — and disagreement with his son over the merits of the mural became so great that they agreed never to discuss this topic at the dinner table!! (Scott interview, 28 February 1980.)

[15] Pijoan in *Student Life*, 23 March 1937.

[16] *Student Life*, 25 April 1930. According to Thomas Beggs (interview 5 March 1980), Pijoan was an exciting and popular if unorthodox and undisciplined instructor, who had continual problems with the Administration during his seven years at Pomona. The **Prometheus** mural apparently represented the last straw to the administration. This memo (dated 26 March 1930: from the College Controller to President

Edmunds) indicates the administration's view of Pijoan:

In the light of Mr. Pijoan's remarks at the College Club yesterday and a conference with Mr. Webber it seems to me essential that we protect ourselves by requiring a cartoon in color showing the fresco proposed before any work in Frary Hall is permitted. Experience with Mr. Pijoan's taste in the past is such as to make it imperative in my judgment.

[17] Johnson letter quoted in *Student Life*, 1 May 1930.

[18] Alma Reed letter to Dr. Alvin Johnson, dated 28 April 1931, generously made available to me by Dr William B. Scott, who is presently writing a history of the New School. In this letter Reed also cites the months Orozco worked in California 'without financial compensation.' Curiously, in her biography Reed does not mention her patronage of the mural.

[19] a. Reed, Orozco, p.208. For their part the New School asked Orozco and Thomas Hart Benton (who also painted murals at the New School at this time) to '*paint a subject he regarded as of such importance that no history written a hundred years from now could fail to devote a chapter to it*' ('Notes on the New School Murals', Alvin Johnson; New School publication, n.d.).
b. At the 'Ashram', named after Gandhi's dwelling at Wardha, Reed and her friends discussed the state of the world in decorous fashion (Reed, *Orozco*, p.35-36):
Over preserved orange blossoms and rose-flavored Turkish coffee... we discussed mankind's chances for stemming the blood-red rivers of internecine strife. We talked about the pacifist doctrines of the world's great teachers — Jesus and Buddha, Lao-Tze, Zoroaster, Walt Whitman, Emerson, and Gandhi. We exchanged ideas as to how these doctrines might be applied to the emerging conflicts of our own time in ways that would be both consistent with the highest ideals of civilized behavior and realistic in their approach to the activistic impulses and groups.

Footnotes continued on p.127

J.C.Orozco

The Orozco Frescoes at Dartmouth

Foreword to a booklet published by Dartmouth College on the murals in 1934

In every painting, as in any other work of art, there is always an IDEA, never a STORY. The idea is the point of departure, the first cause of the plastic construction, and it is present all the time as energy-creating matter. The stories and other literary associations exist only in the mind of the spectator, the painting acting as the stimulus.

There are many literary associations as spectators. One of them, when looking at a picture representing a scene of war, for example, may start thinking of murder, another of pacifism, another of anatomy, another of history, and so on. Consequently, to write a story and to say that it is actually TOLD by a painting is wrong and untrue. Now the ORGANIC IDEA of every painting, even the worst in the world, is extremely obvious to the average spectator with normal mind and normal sight. The artist cannot possibly hide it. It might be a poor, superfluous and ridiculous idea or a great and significant one.

But the important point regarding the frescoes of Baker Library is not only the quality of the idea that initiates and organises the whole structure, it is also the fact that it is an AMERICAN idea developed into American forms, American feeling, and, as a consequence, into American style.

It is unnecessary to speak about TRADITION. Certainly we have to fall in line and learn our lesson from the masters. If there is another way it has not been discovered yet. It seems that the line of culture is continuous, without shortcuts, unbroken FROM THE UNKNOWN BEGINNING TO THE UNKNOWN END. But we are proud to say now: This is no imitation, this is our OWN effort, to the limit of our own strength and experience, in all sincerity and spontaneity.

1934 ▶

Ancient Human Sacrifice

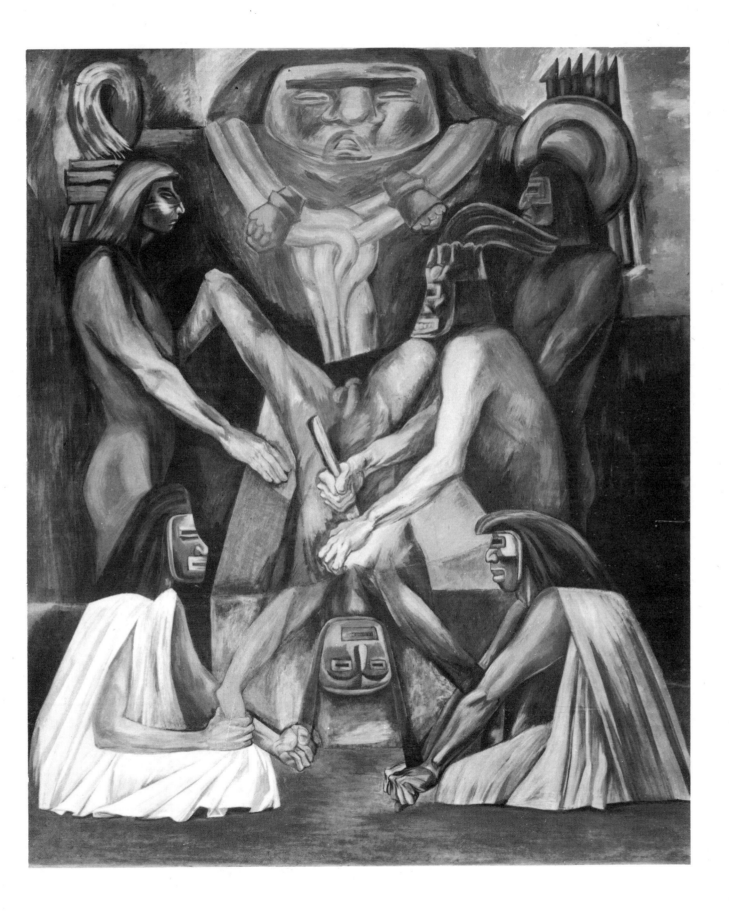

61

The Coming of Quetzalcoatl

The Departure of Quetzalcoatl

Above,
**The Pre-Columbian
Golden Age**

**Cortez
and the Cross**

**Below,
Anglo-America**

The Machine

Below, **Gods of the Modern World**

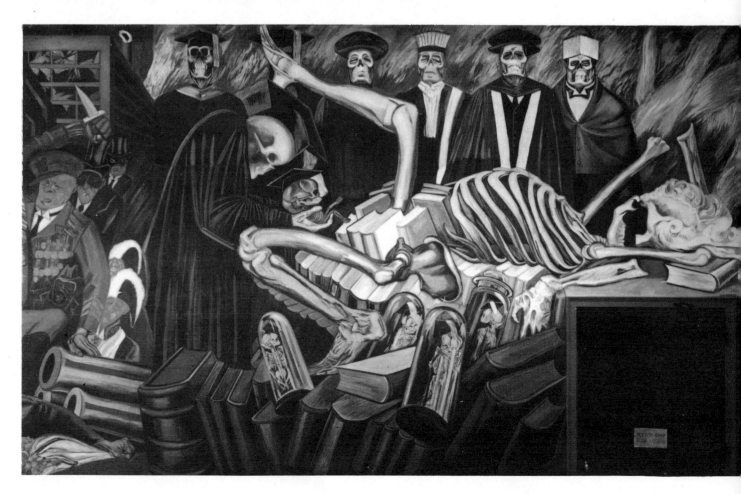

Modern Industrial Man

Modern Human Sacrifice

Sergei Eisenstein

Orozco: The Prometheus of Mexican Painting[1]
[Notes]

'There are as many literary associations as spectators'
From Orozco's introduction to the booklet *The Orozco Frescoes at Dartmouth* Hanover NH 1934

'Let these be mine!' — Eisenstein

● It is ridiculous to talk of Apollo when we look at the Rabelaisian, fat-bellied figure of Diego, his flesh bursting out from overtight trousers and his greasy skin appearing tightly stretched from his face to his stomach.

It is equally difficult to think of Dionysus in referring to an individual [Orozco] of Promethean proportions (it is no accident that Prometheus is the subject of one of his frescoes), protected by enormous round glasses with lenses as thick as the portholes of the extraordinary Captain Nemo's submarine Nautilus, as related in Jules Verne's marvellous stories.

Perhaps it is both difficult *and* ridiculous, but this trivial antithesis of Apollo and Dionysus has nevertheless materialised in its own paradoxical way into the delirious murals of these two colourful figures.

Their intensity is distinct. Quantitive in Diego. Qualitative in Orozco.

Square kilometres in area in the one, and so much explosive energy in the other.

The static quality of Diego. Mrs Bloom of *Ulysses* dashed to the ground in the fresco 'The breakfast of the Aesthetes'.[2] This reality is displayed, arranged on the surface of the walls. [And] the nerve of reality is fixed, as though with a nail to the wall. A reality is placed on the wall.

A scream on a surface *through* form and *through* style. [Orozco: The Trench]

Three men on a barricade. Only one is balanced on the surface. One flies towards the spectator. The other one, behind his fist, thrusts himself into the depths beyond the barricade which they are defending. The fist, huge in proportion, projects from the wall above the heads of those who draw near to look.

The camp follower is walking out towards the vanishing plains, which are twisted by the fierceness of the agave plants. These edges hurt one's eyes as do the pages of *Los de Abajo* ('The Underdogs' — a novel by Mariano Azuela, illustrated by Orozco). Walls are not painted in this way. Illustrations are not made like this.

This kind of thing is not painted on walls. On the first floor of the Prepatoria, while pasting up Posada's satirical enlargement (an etching) — maidens seeking suitors — who was it who forgot to clear away this chaotic composition — painted in broad strokes as if it were a poster which would be destroyed after a day? It was the same person who, not far away, fixed on the wall the story of the Leper and the philanthropic Friar who kissed the leper on the lips. It was he, the same, who played with the low projecting angles of the walls,

bringing them together in the pictorial image of generous hands and poorboxes; coins, given by the poor, fall into the greasy hands of the priest.

It is not these subjects nor in this way that he [Orozco] should paint on walls. These are not displays of bodies and outlines of machines. It is only an explosion from the surface. The bodies and columns plunge headlong. It is an agglomeration of surfaces. Revolutionary force. Cyclone.

Orozco's progress: Dartmouth. There it was the most terrible. Superhuman passions. Social outcry. And amongst these social caricatures, a handsome young

boy, with that ease which only Americans have, was sitting peacefully reading in that room overflowing with a social tumult of colours. Orozco, at least, is not going to compromise. He does not go down to the Stock Exchange in San Francisco like his Apollonian colleague, who made a crown of laurels for the golden calf of his California — almost Mrs Bloom — almost a self-portrait of Diego!

But I feel apprehension about these surroundings. In the well meaning libraries, where Orozco's street cries seem to echo from behind the lenses of his glasses. These lenses are even thicker than those of Nautilus, and sharpen his social vision like a telescope. Here the surroundings are a barrier against the noise in the street where the class struggles take place. The bookish spirit of sleeping consciences passes without questioning among this poetry of nightmares and horrors, caught in the frames of the bookshelves. This young boy kills me. He seems to be in an aquarium, where whatever hidden horrors, snakes, there are, he is safe behind the glass.

In this way Orozco is encased in glass, audiences contemplate and enjoy social horrors as grand guignol. Horror is neutralised.

Orozco's frescoes ought to wage war out there; ... destroying the old world and directed towards the creating of New Worlds.

Now is the time to replace the beard of the mythical Quetzalcoatl with that of the combative Marx. The sash across the unknown soldier falls allegorically and remotely, softening the horror of the Aztec sacrifice, just as the sacrifice brings the unknown soldier under the cover of something remote and fabulous. No longer the direct, the present. No longer the shock. The combat. The roaring and explosive!

The eyes which look at the works of Orozco push them on to a level far above that of technique or style — the level which the painter himself transcends. They do for him what Diego does for himself. [He is] a painter outside an audience. Orozco ought to be with us.

[1] Eisenstein had met Orozco on one occasion in 1932 and knew the Preparatory School murals well. Early in 1935 he was given by Jay Leyda, a young American student of cinema in Moscow, a copy of the booklet in the Dartmouth murals. Eisenstein liked these murals so much that he began to prepare the above text. It was never completed.

[2] The meaning of the phrase 'Mrs Bloom of *Ulysses* dashed to the ground in the fresco "The breakfast of the Aesthetes"' is obscure but its meaning becomes clear in the first (English) text in which Eisenstein writes about a fresco of Rivera which was in the Ministry of Education:

'*Ulysses* is Joyce's masterpiece, the greatest literary work in the world, which eclipses Rabelais, Balzac and Dante. Joyce's masterpiece thrown to the ground in the assembly of decadents. I know that this is a glove thrown down by Diego to those who are not body and soul with the best that there is in Mexico.'

Immediately afterwards, Eisenstein compares the creative method of Rivera (his 'symbolic self-portrait') with the last chapter of *Ulysses* — the inner monologue of Molly Bloom.

'... walk another hour in the gallery of Education covered with the forms and the faces of Diego Rivera. And suddenly, do they not seem in some way identical, similar to an uninterrupted current in the monologue — without commas, full stops, without colour — in the last chapter of *Ulysses* ... the monologue of Mrs Leopold Bloom ... ?

At some moment they seem to begin to glow in a splendid multicoloured river not destructive like lava, but highly coloured like Nature, which mysteriously emerges in the period of spring and fertility, when vitality changes from one form to another and appears again in an infinite diversity of new forms and new creations ...'

'Mrs Bloom, is moreover, another thing: Mother Earth. Her perpetual fertility, is the most powerful feeling personified ...'

'To Mother Earth, to the Mother of all earthly things, I would compare Diego, who peoples his ark with an endless exodus of animals of human image, and human beings subjected to an animal exploitation. The womb could be the symbol of the infinite creative capacity of this man.'

Translation by Anne Pears and Olbeth Rossi

Winter, oil on canvas, 1932 (cat.59)

Catharsis:
Mural in the Palace of Fine Arts,
Mexico City,
1934

Total area 50 sq. metres

The University of Guadalajara
Creative Man and the People and its False Leaders
Murals in the Assembly Hall, 1936

Total area 430 sq. metres

Left-hand page: **The Leaders** (side panel)
Right-hand page: General view of murals
on cupola and stage
colour illustrations on pp.40,41,44,45

A Terrible Beauty: Orozco's Murals in Guadalajara 1936-1939

● The work of a muralist is by its nature dispersed and, depending upon the will of patrons, works which are closely related in time or theme are often located in different cities or even different countries. Guadalajara, capital of the state of Jalisco, is an exception to this. It was truly fortunate to host Orozco during one of the most intensely creative periods of his life, and in return received three cycles of murals which, when viewed together, must form the most important work he ever made. They were commissioned by Don Everado Topete, the state governor of Jalisco.

Orozco had strong links with Guadalajara for not only was it the capital of the state in which he had been born in 1883, but he had also spent his early childhood there from 1885 to 1890. He intermittently returned to Guadalajara throughout his life and the studio home which he built there is now a museum dedicated to his memory.

The cycles that Orozco created in the city are found in three separate buildings. The first, started in 1936, is in the Assembly Hall of the city's university. The second, started in 1937, is over the staircase of the Palace of Government, while the third and the most ambitious of the three is in the deconsecrated chapel of the Hospicio Cabañas, formerly the city's orphanage. This he painted between the years of 1938 and 1939.[1]

Orozco was quite unlike his two great compatriots Rivera and Siqueiros in that he kept his distance, both from them and from the movement to which they all belonged. Both Rivera and Siqueiros in their murals concerned themselves with the celebration of humanity's struggle to achieve freedom and dignity. But Orozco was captivated and absorbed by what he saw as the stark reality of human existence, of man's apparent inability to realise his most noble aspirations or to live with others in freedom and liberty. Orozco believed passionately in the sanctity of freedom but when he looked around him, in spite of the 'progress' of the 20th century, he saw oppression and slavery. Man's social systems seemed specifically designed to oppress rather than govern.

The glaring disparity between ideals on the one hand and oppressive reality on the other proved to be the vital central theme in his work. It was in the Guadalajara murals that his treatment of this developed and reached its most intense expression. Orozco's stance was quite separate from that of the other leading muralists: the ideal of freedom for him could not be gained by joining a political party of the left, as did Rivera, Siqueiros and others.[2] And indeed throughout his life his position had been one of a deeply committed non-alignment. But he was far from being the anarchist that some of his critics suggested and vehemently rejected such charges:

'Those who say I am an anarchist do not know

me. I am a partisan with absolute freedom of thought a real free thinker; neither a dogmatist nor an anarchist; neither an enemy of hierarchies nor a partisan of unyielding affirmations.' [3]

In his examination of freedom as an ideal in his work Orozco expressed himself in ways which many found, to say the least, contradictory. Practically every writer on Orozco has commented on this. And these apparent contradictions have generated much confusion. Antonio Rodrigues for example wrote: *'To some he appears as a reactionary, or as a Catholic; to others a communist or an atheist. Some see him as a prophet, others a confused thinker unable to see the false from the true.'* [4]

But the contradictions within Orozco's work are dialectical and calculated. They are not confused, and are neither dogmatic nor monolithic. Idealism, with its aspirations towards liberty and freedom, is posed inevitably against the stark reality of exploitation, tyranny, hypocrisy and falseness. Wherever he detected greed, venality, corruption or hypocrisy, wherever he saw the call for freedom being traded for a tarnished imposter, he brought a ruthless criticism to bear on its usurpers — however fine their rhetoric and however pure the colour of their banners. For him the critique of reality was a **'penetrating mission of the spirit and an expressive capacity in art.'**

Yet this penchant for sharp criticism of the social world was only one side of the dual position that he held, for he accepted both what was good in man and what was bad. **'I accept these characteristics'** he wrote, **'as forming part of a unity. In everything, in men and in things I believe there are good and bad sides. It is in this way the artist must face the problems which he utilises as raw material for his works.'** Within these unities and polarities lie the core of Orozco's philosophical position. The murals at Guadalajara are the most complete and quintessential reflection and expression of these and are the most significant works by one of the leading philosophical painters of our time.

In the first two cycles of murals, the University Assembly Hall and the Government Palace, Orozco dealt largely with contemporary issues: the struggles, betrayal and loss of direction of the masses were set against a more cerebral, ideal view.

In the third cycle, that in the former chapel of the Hospicio Cabañas, Orozco expressed similar dualities but set against the tableau of the historical and cultural development of Mexico. This development was shown specifically in terms of the metamorphosis brought about by the absorption of the Indian past at the hands of the Spanish Conquest, but also, in this case, Mexican history served as an allegory of a much wider experience. In the cupola of the former chapel lies the apotheosis of this work: here in the **The Man of Fire** lies a dramatic if enigmatic response to the sombre images he had depicted below.

In all of the Guadalajara murals there is a marked physical isolation of opposed points of view. In each case the lower sections contain material that is often severe, critical, pessimistic and sometimes nihilistic. This is the world of human experience. The upper sections on the other hand have a totally different feel: they express the affirmative, the inspirational and the idealistic. They are the domain of human ideals, intellect and hopes.

This polarity in conception between the upper and lower sections of each cycle is also reflected in the way Orozco approached them as a painter. The lower sections are, for the most part, austere in colour, which in the first two cycles tends towards the monochromatic. Acidic greys highlighted with flecks of white describe the figures. The drawing is satirical, gestural and expressionistic, conveying an atmosphere of critical anger and bitterness. On the other hand, the upper reaches of the cycles contain drawing that is much calmer, more monumental and classical. Likewise the colour, becomes brighter, and more brilliant in tone — reflecting the thematic change of emphasis.

Orozco's dualistic approach is similarly reflected throughout the development of his imagery at this time. In this, the transmutation of the machine into a human or animal torso is of particular importance. This image, which appears also in his easel painting and graphic work can be found in some of the large vaulted panels over the nave in the Hospicio Cabañas. Here the machine torso expresses the aggressive and technically advanced character of the Conquest. It was an image that for Orozco evoked the spirit of the modern age — a spirit cast into a mould of mechanical and unfeeling aggression.

The cascades of rifles, the stacks of books — open and closed — and the billowing red flags are also important images. In the first cycle at Guadalajara the rifles and books are used satirically. Here, rather than being a symbol of knowledge, the book represents blind dogmatism — secondary knowledge. The rifles contextualise the character of this stupidity. The meaning of the image of the red flag changed according to its context: it could be used in either a negative or positive way. It is for example an emblem of solidarity, democracy, of nobility of purpose in the cupola of the University, whilst on the staircase of the Government Palace it expresses the opposite — tyranny, exploitation and cruelty — it is literally portrayed as a blindfold.[7]

But perhaps most important and impressive of all the motifs used by Orozco in Guadalajara is the image of fire. A raging conflagration is in the background to the lower mural in the University Assembly Hall; a firebrand is a central image on the staircase of the Governmental Palace and flames lick through the mass of struggling figures below; but most disconcertingly, in a symbolic evocation of human conflict, fire consumes totally a figure of a man in the cupola of the Hospicio Cabañas. Fire — an apocalyptic symbol of pain,

purification, conflict and inspiration — was a central motif throughout the whole of Orozco's mature work.

The **Man of Fire** had also been the central image in the mural **Prometheus** made some nine years previously at Pomona College in California. The symbol of fire had previously appeared in certain sections of the murals in Dartmouth College library in New Hampshire, made 1932-34, as well as in the panel **Catharsis**, 1934, at the Palace of Fine Arts in Mexico City. But although such images recur, their meaning is heavily dependent upon their context within each cycle. In the light of this, it is relevant to examine each of the Guadalajara cycles more closely.

The first, in the Assembly Hall of the University, was started by Orozco in 1936. It is comprised of two separate murals, one high up in the enormous cupola that dominates the room, the other in the walled niche behind the speaker's dias. The cupola fresco is entitled **Creative Man** and depicts a synthesis of man's most noble qualities in the form of images of the Worker, the Philosopher-Teacher, the Scientist, and the Rebel. These four large figures are arranged against a deep red background and occupy the whole area of the cupola. The scientist, whose head faces in several directions simultaneously, is a straightforward representation of the inquiring, human mind seeking out knowledge through discovery and invention. The figure of the Worker — technical and constructive man — appears to emanate from a strange hooked machine complex, while in his hand he clasps a lever. In the relationship

The Worker,
detail from **Creative Man**

75

Right and overleaf: **The Masses**
Details from **Hidalgo and National Independence**
Palace of Government, Guadalajara, 1937-38

between the other figures, the Philosopher-Teacher and the Rebel, Orozco postulates an ideal unity between thought and action.[9] The Rebel, whose body projects down strongly towards the viewer, is shown constrained by a rope around his neck — a symbol of his oppression. In one of his hands he holds a large swirling red flag which flows over to form the backdrop to the raised didactic gesture of the Philosopher-Teacher. The clasped hands of the Rebel and the Philosopher, just visible at the edge of the cupola, cement this unity of thought and action — the physical and intellectual aspects of progress.

But in the mural below, Orozco expresses the duality of thought and action in a completely different way, expressing the realm not of human ideals but of human experience. **The Rebellion of Man** — the title of the whole mural — represents the rebellion of the masses against their exploiters.

Knife and Book, Detail from **The Rebellion of Man** 1936

The presentation of this angry theme is subdivided into three constituent parts. Each part occupies a separate panel of the niche and conveys its own subject and character, which Orozco uses in an almost Brechtian way to play off against the adjoining panels. The central panel — **The People and its False Leaders** — some 30 feet square — is the introduction to the theme. Against a background of flames, Orozco has placed a mass of emaciated and wretched people. In anger and desperation they gesticulate at a group of men to their left — the ideologues of revolution. In the two narrow adjoining panels showing the wretched suffering and the corrupt leaders, Orozco presents the basis for this anger. In the left hand panel — **The Leaders** — three ugly, ape-like figures represent the presence of a new set of brutish power-seeking 'Caudillos' — a consequence of false leadership and a pretext for revolt. In their military uniform and workmens' overalls they caricature the new military and labour leadership of the Revolution. Their swaggering stance and menacing sledgehammers together with the pile of books and rifles at their side suggest the imposition by brute force of the ideologies contained in the books.

Certainly it seems by the physical attributes of the front pair of figures that Orozco intended it to be a criticism, not of organised labour as such, but of some of its leaders.[10] However since the presentation is not a literal one his criticism should perhaps be taken on a

general rather than on a specific level. Nevertheless, the mural is inescapably as much a comment on the failure of the Mexican Revolution as it is a philosophical thesis on the dilemma contained within revolutionary struggle in general. By the late '20s and early '30s corruption and reaction were characteristics of the Mexican political scene and some labour leaders, tolerated by their military allies, had betrayed their followers for their own gain. Orozco knew this well and this work can be seen as a seering indictment.

Detail from **The Victims,** 1936
University of Guadalajara

This indictment is most expressively invoked in the panel called **The Victims** at the right hand of the lower mural. The three emaciated figures shown there are victims not only of false leadership but also of the betrayal of their revolt. In the cold grey of their bodies and in the leaden, murky red background Orozco emphasises their wretchedness. He does not romanticise the depiction of their suffering but uses it in a calculated way to drive home the consequences of the central theme of the murals.

The theme of contemporary revolt was one that Orozco repeated in the next cycle. But here, on the walls over the staircase of the Government Palace, the principal subject was more specifically Mexican — the famous Jesuit priest, Miguel Hidalgo, who as a champion of the Indian, the poor and the oppressed had in 1810 been the leader of an uprising against Spanish rule.[11] His name had become synonymous in the minds of every Mexican with their struggle for independence, freedom and justice. But although a Mexican subject was obviously more fitting for a regional centre of government, this did not limit the relevance of the mural's theme and statement. Indeed, apart from the figure of Hidalgo there is no other specifically Mexican reference in this work.

The cycle is painted around three very large adjoining walls above a staircase. At their top these walls converge in a sweeping curve that then drops down towards a series of arched entrances to an upper floor corridor. The figure of Hidalgo occupies the whole of the upper part of the central wall, where, having risen vertically from its base, it arches over the staircase. The effect of this is to present Hidalgo as a giant, physically

dominating the whole area below him. Below Hidalgo is a picture of a cataclysmic conflict: a hoard of emaciated figures are seen bludgeoning and knifing each other to death amongst a sea of red flags and flames. The conflict brings total confusion and despair in its train.

On the walls to the right and left Orozco has placed images that give a context to this confusion. On the left hand wall, entitled **The Phantasms of Religion in Alliance with the Military,** set against a deep red background summarize the dark, mystical, demonic and reactionary forces of the clerical and military Establishment. It is a reference to the historical role played by these forces in Mexican history. On the right hand wall in **Carnival of the Ideologies** Orozco placed a highly satirical depiction of the conflicting philosophies of the 20th century.

The enormous figure of Hidalgo and the cataclysmic struggle below him is basically a reinterpretation of the idea contained within the relationship between the Philosopher-Teacher figure and the Rebel in the Assembly Hall cupola. But instead of calmness, Hidalgo suggests a messianic urgency; the calm didactic gesture of the Philosopher-Teacher has now been transformed into a raised clenched fist reminiscent of that of Christ in Michelangelo's *Last Judgment*. In the place of the gently touching hands the relationship between Hidalgo and the rebellious masses below is characterised in the image of the firebrand which he violently thrusts out towards their struggle.

The images of **The Carnival of the Ideologies** and **The Phantasms of Religion in Alliance with the Military** are used in a similar way to those of the book-wielding ideologues and their brutish leaders on the side panels in the mural in the Assembly Hall. In each they appear both as the confusers and the oppressors of the people.

One other image which is notable for its transformation in this cycle is the red flag that covers the face of the military figure of the left hand panel. It is obviously intended to have the very opposite meaning to its counterpart in the cupola of the Assembly Hall, and is an echo of a very similar image in one of Orozco's much earlier murals: **The Revolutionary Trinity,** 1926, in the National Preparatory School in Mexico City. Both imply a blindness and loss of direction in the Revolution — despotism and betrayal triumph.

For Orozco the images on the left and right hand walls clearly sum up the historical and contemporary forces that have distorted and diverted the cause which Hidalgo represented. Hidalgo is now seen, despite his messianic purity as an idealistic instigator and catalyst in a rebellion and struggle that has now found itself lost in despair and confusion.

The gigantic and towering figure of Hidalgo is used by Orozco as a symbol of revolutionary fervour and it is significant that he was to depict him in a very different way. Much later in his life in 1948, on the ceiling of the Chamber of Deputies, also in the Government palace in Guadalajara. In this later version, Hidalgo is depicted

Right: **Hidalgo and National Independence**
Overleaf: **The Carnival of the Ideologies**
Both murals on the main staircase, Palace of Government,
Guadalajara, 1937-38

not so much as a messianic symbol, but as a more reflective, perhaps apprehensive, leader. He is surrounded by figures of slaves — the past, the present and the future — who reach out their manacled and cruelly bound heads and hands towards him.[12] The title of this mural is **The Great Mexican Revolutionary Legislation and the Abolition of Slavery.**

In the final cycle of the 1936-39 period, at the Hospicio Cabañas, Orozco undertook his most physically ambitious project, covering over 1200 square metres of wall with fresco. In plan the building is cruciform with a large cupola over the intersection. The painted surfaces within the building consist of the cupola, the vaulted panels along each side of the aisle and a number of smaller areas.

Thematically the whole cycle expresses the duality of the human character within a view of the evolution of Mexican society. Orozco was able to depict the character of the metamorphosis which his country had undergone at the hands of the Spanish Conquest. As with the earlier cycles, he counterposed his often harsh view of actual experience, here expressed through his country's history, with an affirmation of the ideals and capabilities of the human spirit. The former he represented in the vaults and aisle panels over and around the nave and the transept, while the latter he confined to the area of the magnificient cupola.

In formulating a view on the historical transformation of his country, Orozco avoided a merely simplistic sequential or episodic transcription of events. Such was not his method, for his purpose was to put forward, through the building up and juxtaposing of images and scenes, an overall picture that showed the dual character of that development — both its positive and negative features. It was an approach to history that, as the writer Bernard Myers has pointed out, was in a sense didactic, working towards a humanistic ideal.[13] In doing this Orozco, as ever, avoided a polarised view. He did not unquestioningly espouse the cause of pre-Hispanic Indian Mexico, nor did he view the Spanish Conquest as a civilising advancement of a harsh and backward Indian world. In Orozco's mind the polarity of that which was good or bad in his country's history was not dictated by culture, race or time.

Taken as a whole the images that Orozco created in the panels of the vaults, transepts, and aisle very

Detail: Hidalgo,
Chamber of Deputies, 1948

roughly fall into four sections. Within each section the images were ordered to build up a general picture of an historical evolution.

The panels within the east and west transepts show the cruel and barbaric world of ancient Indian Mexico, with its bloody sacrifices and macabre rituals; they also contain images of Franciscan monks as well as of Indian and Spanish warriors. Together these images introduce an historical moment and its protagonists: an Indian world about to be transformed by military and spiritual means. The dual character of this impending transformation is continued and expanded in the panels in the northern end of the nave and in the vaults.

In the huge panels in the vaults Orozco expresses the character of the Conquest at its most harsh. Here the Indian world is crushed and transformed by European Renaissance man at his most aggressive, acquisitive and violent. The subjugation of the Indian appears total and final. In their composite images each panel in the vault builds up a picture of this plunder and transformation. In one of these the image of the Spanish King Philip II supporting a cross and a crown presents the very foundation of the conquest: the monarchy and the catholic faith. In another, a twin headed horse with a rider encased in armour is shown charging and smashing its way through multitudes of vanquished Indian warriors.[14] This military evocation of the subjugation of the Indian is strangely echoed in a following panel showing his spiritual transformation. Here a Franciscan priest holds over the head of a kneeling Indian a crucifix whose edges are sharpened like a sword. At the priest's side is a banner carrying the first letters of the European alphabet. Together these arranged images vividly express the character of this cultural and spiritual transformation — the ruthless imposition of an evangelical and literary faith. The spiritual turmoil between the two cultures of this time is expressively depicted in the image of another panel where the heads of the gods and prophets of the two cultures converge around a naked torso.

The Phantasms of Religion in Support of the Military,
Palace of Government, Guadalajara, 1937-8

In the panels in the northern part of the nave Orozco develops and integrates images of machines into the new Mexico. In two of the panels the machine expresses the idea of the Conquest as a symbol of modern war, what the writer Salvador Echavarría described as 'The first war enterprise of great scope in the scientific era'.[15] In the image of the **Mechanical Horse** Orozco creates a visual metaphor for the conquistadorial horse as a modern battle tank. Upon its grotesquely mechanical back and body there appears, in a banner, the image of the heraldic lion and tower of Castile. Its position is precisely that of a battle tank turret. In this mechanical monster Orozco had created a sinister caricature of Don Quixote's famous horse Rozinante, but here its rider follows not the noble ideal of justice, but the cause of death and destruction. The image of Hernan Cortez, the leader of the Conquistadores, extends this metaphor. He is clad in armour, and his body with its nuts and bolts and pistons has taken on the appearance of a machine.

But Orozco does show more positive benefits from the Conquest. In the panels of the aisle below, in the northern end of the nave, he presents images which depict the development of culture and architecture. European architecture is shown fusing with that of the Indian world, and in the wall panels above the nave doors portraits of the painter El Greco and the writer Cervantes are incorporated into the schema. At the southern end of the nave, Orozco made images of the spiritual legacy of the Conquest. Evoking the tradition of the Franciscan monks, the concept of Charity and help for the poor is shown in the guise of the portrait of Bishop Juan Ruíz de Cabañas, the founder of the Orphanage. But this faces images of faceless contemporary despotism. In three sombre grey panels Orozco shows a world in which individuality and freedom are suppressed. The Masses are mechanised and moved forward in inhuman unison. It is true that in this cycle Orozco had already expressed the cruelty and tyranny of Indians and Conquistadores but it is the present that seems the most threatening. Orozco was of course right in believing this as these panels were painted during the world political crisis of 1938-39.

Yet this is not Orozco's final comment. For high up in the cupola of the building is **The Man of Fire** — an apotheosis or an apocalypse? Around the edge of the cupola three figures form a circular foreground to a mass of flames. Their circular composition echoes the figures in that of the University cupola as well as those in many 17th-century Italian ceiling paintings. As in the 17th-century compositions, these figures introduce the motif of 'ascension', for engulfed in the middle of these flames is a burning human form. But this figure is hard to read, it is both disintegrating and seems to rise like a phoenix from the ashes. The image is enigmatic and, characteristically, Orozco himself did not indicate how it should be read; like the other central images examined above it has both a positive and negative aspect. It is in part a metaphor for the theme of social struggle — the central theme of this and the other murals in Guadalajara; partly also the chimera of the ideal. Like Hidalgo's torch it destroys, enlightens and purifies to enable a new start.

Certainly it is an image of regeneration and it is wholly consistent that Orozco should in the end affirm his belief in the irrepressibility of the human soul regardless of the cruelties and horrors meted out to it.

In this his final apotheosis at Guadalajara, Orozco concluded the work of the most productive and significant period of his life. Over all it is an uncompromising expression of a painter who had seen his country's revolution '*stop halfway tired and abandoned by its supporters*'.[16] If his strictures on the fallibility of human beings seemed to some unnecessarily harsh or his view of the revolution too one sided then it is because Orozco believed in **'boldness of thinking, in speaking out about things as one feels them in the moment of speaking; in having the temerity to proclaim what one believes to be true without fear of the consequences.'**[17] But above all else the importance of the work at Guadalajara lies in the complete synthesis between Orozco the thinker and Orozco the painter. His biographer and friend Luis Cardoza y Aragón was never more accurate than when he wrote '*Those who do not know Orozco at Guadalajara do not know Orozco.*'[18]

[1]Orozco's fees for these murals were:
Assembly Hall   430 sq.m 10,000 pesos
Government Palace
  Staircase   430 sq.m 12,000 pesos
Hospicio Cabañas 1250 sq.m 70,000 pesos
[2]Siqueiros, Rivera and O'Higgins were members of the Mexican Communist Party.
[3]From a Declaration published in *Tiempo*, Mexico D. F. September 1946 No.13. In *La Pintura Mural de la Revolucion Mexicana*, Fondo Editorial de la Plastica Mexicana, Mexico DF, 1975, 2nd edition, p. 192.
[4]A. Rodrigues, *History of Mexican Mural Painting*, London, 1969, p. 355.
[5]La Pintura Mural *op. cit.* p. 192.
[6]Ibid. p. 200.
[7]The red flag also appears as a blindfold in the panel *Revolutionary Trinity* 1926 in the National Preparatory School, Mexico City.
[8]The diameter of the cupola is 14 metres
[9]The face of the Philosopher-Teacher is

The Hospicio Cabañas, Guadalajara: Frescoes, 1938-39

Mexico Before and After the Spanish Conquest, Man and the urge to better himself

Total area 1250 sq.metres

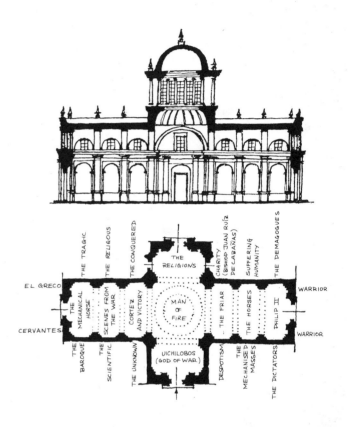

reputed to be modelled on that of Vicente Lombardo Toledano who had commissioned Orozco's first murals whilst director of the National Preparatory School in Mexico City in 1923. During the Cárdenas Presidency, 1934-40, he was a well respected labour leader.

[10]Orozco may have had in mind the Trade Union boss Luis Morones whom he had previously satirised in a biting caricature. During the early '30s Morones was head of the Confederacion Regional Obrera Mexicana (a major labour organisation) and was dismissed for corruption. Also one of the false leaders in the central panel does have more than a passing resemblance to Karl Marx.

[11]As the parish priest of the small town of Dolores, Hidalgo had called his people in the famous 'Grito Dolores' to rise up and fight the Spanish.

[12]Orozco also treated the theme of Slaves in a series of powerful easel paintings. Cats: 171-178.

[13]B. Myers, *Mexican Art in Our Time*, New York, 1956, p. 158.

[14]The horse was unknown to the Indian before the Conquest. When they first saw a mounted horse, they thought horse and rider were the same animal and therefore that the horse had two heads.

[15]S. Echavarría, *Jalisco en el Arte*, Mexico DF, 1973, p. 32.

[16]A. Rodrigues, *op. cit*, p. 56.

[17]McKinley Helm, *Man of Fire. J. C. Orozco an interpretive memoir*, Boston, 1953. p. 109.

[18]Luis Cardoza y Aragón, *Mexican Art Today*, Mexico City, 1966, p. 37.

Dedicatory wall panel showing the building, Hospicio Cabañas

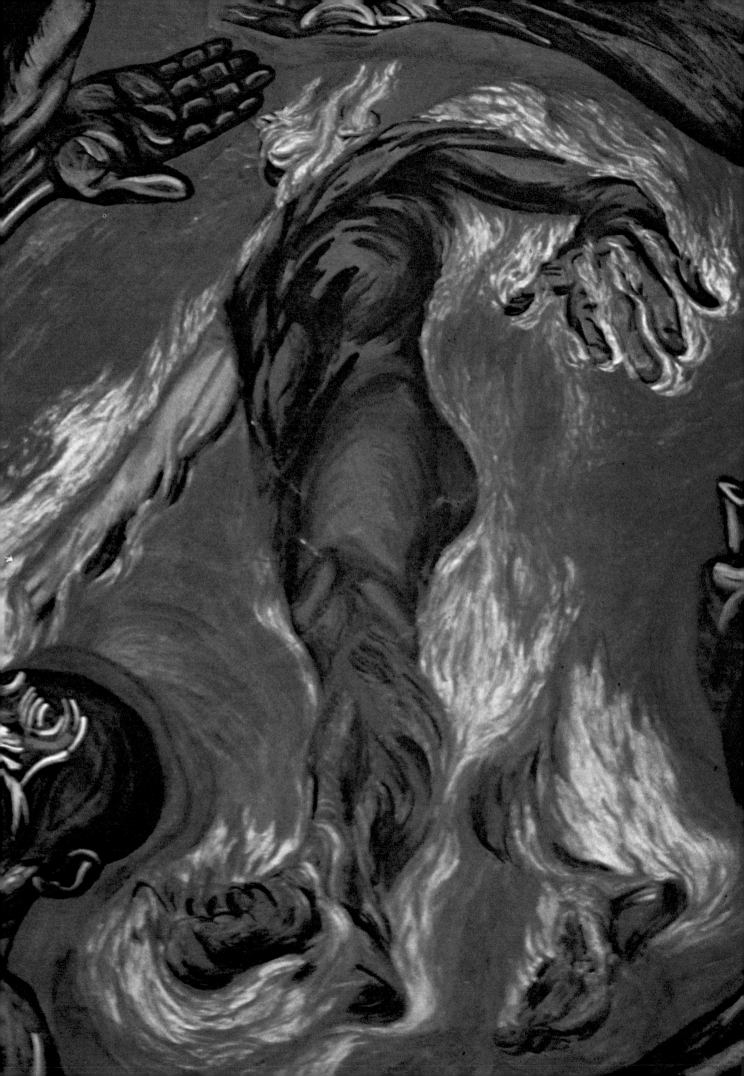

Frescoes from the ceiling of the Hospicio Cabañas, Guadalajara, 1938-39:
Below, **Philip II;** opposite, top, **The Horses;** below, **The Mechanical Horse**

The Tyrant
oil and tempera on canvas, 1947
(cat.142)

Demagogue
oil and tempera on canvas, 1946
(cat.141)

National Allegory, 1947-48:
the Open-Air Lecture Theatre,
National School of Teachers,
Mexico City

Total area 380 sq. metres

Overleaf:
left, **Despotism** 1938-39
right, **The Dictators**
1938-39
Hospicio Cabañas
Guadalajara

Metaphysical Landscape
piroxiline on masonite, 1948
(cat.203)

David Elliott
A New Poetry: Orozco's Work 1940-1949

● After the universality and the painterly expressionism
of the murals in the Hospicio Cabañas, one can see a
distinct change in tone in the predominantly black and
white mural cycle in the Gabino Ortiz Library in
Jiquilpan which Orozco painted the following year in
1940. The Library was converted from a nineteenth-
century chapel which accounts for the long high walls
and the dominant apse. The drawings on the side walls
all depict scenes from the time of the Mexican
Revolution, some of them connected with Jiquilpan
itself, whilst on the end wall, facing the observer as he
enters the room, is an **Allegory of Mexico.** In this
Orozco has used colour broadly, whereas in the side
walls colour is used only as an accent — the red flags in
The Masses for example. The symbolism of the
Allegory also contrasts strongly with the starkness and
realism of the other scenes. Justino Fernandez, critic,
friend and biographer of Orozco described the Allegory
in this way:

   *'Orozco has projected here his concept of the Mexican —
the painful, slow advance, the violence, the drama and
dignity, evil and greatness; this human comedy —
pretension without substance, religiosity without religion —
and, undefiled, the true national conscience.'*

   The side panels show a range of images: scenes of
exploitation and generalised struggle (**the Overseers,
Brute Forces, The Battle, After the Battle**); two
parodies of the mindlessness and malleability of the
demonstrating masses (these were derived from
drawings and lithographs made some five years
previously for the **Suite Mexicana**) and lastly two
scenes based on historical events around Jiquilpan.
These were **The Shooting of General Alvirez**
commemorating an event which took place in the
nearby town of Guaracha in 1914 and **The Execution
of Madero's Followers** which had taken place in the
following year.

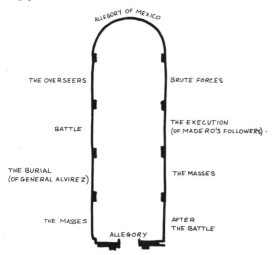

Murals in the Gabino Ortiz Library, Jiquilpan:
From the top, **The Overseers, Battle,
The Burial** (of General Alvirez),
and After the Battle

General view of the Gabino Ortiz Library, Jiquilpan

The subject matter in this cycle was more specific, the scale less ambitious than Cabañas. The Allegory was the first of a series of three he was to carry out during the 1940s. The fact that Orozco was now asked to do this kind of work shows the extent to which he had become accepted within Mexico as one of her greatest painters.

After completing these murals, which took five months, in that same year Orozco returned to New York to paint the six panel mural **Dive Bomber and Tank** for the Museum of Modern Art. It was to coincide with an exhibition entitled *Twenty Centuries of Mexican Art*. He worked on the fresco while the exhibition was open and visitors were able to see its progress; it took him ten days to complete with the help of one assistant. While he was doing this the Museum made a photographic documentation on the work.

Dive Bomber and Tank, which looks back in scale to **Catharsis** of 1934, was essentially a new departure; it represents a serious questioning of his previous methods and it is the first of a series of poetic abstractions from reality which were to be an outstanding feature of his work in the 1940s. The **Man of Fire** was an ultimate statement: conventional imagery could not be charged with greater intensity. Orozco had to look for other forms and other means of expression. **'A painting is a poem and nothing else.'** This was the opening sentence of his description of the **Dive Bomber**. He had made it in six individual panels, each nine feet by three feet, and, while obviously they were painted in a particular order, he maintained that there was to be no set sequence — the order could be mixed up, some panels omitted and others stood on their heads. On the inside back pages of

Orozco working on **Dive Bomber,** 1940

First sketch for **Dive Bomber**

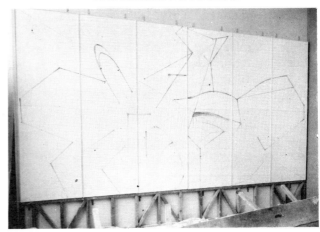

the booklet produced by the Museum about the mural Orozco put forward six different 'preferred' arrangements for the panels. But the idea of interchangeability, in this case, was not synonymous with randomness. The simple geometrical forms upon which the composition was based were distributed along a diagonal axis rising from the bottom right hand corner to the top left. To some extent there was a natural equilibrium which could withstand a displacement in the original linear rhythm. The subject matter of the mural was homogeneous: on the left was a production line of identical bars — reminscent of the **Mechanised Masses** in Cabañas — above these a bomb-like shape thrust upwards whilst below, in three consecutive panels, large heads — reminiscent of huge Olmec carvings — are manacled by chains. In one a rivet is driven through an eye, in the next the lips and nose are stapled together, in the last an iron bar is fastened across the ears.

Orozco working on **Dive Bomber,** 1940

Before Orozco had moved north to New York, President Cárdenas had asked him to make murals in the Supreme Court of Justice in Mexico City. He now, in 1941, returned to Mexico to complete this cycle. The Murals are situated on a large landing at the top of the main flight of stairs in the Court Building; the two side walls were pierced by doors and badly lit, the facing end wall was well lit from the side, the last mural was awkwardly placed on the wall over the stair well. The two side murals are a pair: **Justice** and **False Justice.** Justice is an avenging angel striking down corruption. False Justice is represented by the archetypal image of Justice herself but, instead of balancing the scales, she is asleep, slumped in her chair, whilst below charlatans and crooks flourish. The end wall consists of a symbolical allegory entitled **National Wealth.** Mexican images such as the skull, the skeleton, the jaguar, the indian gods were brought together as symbols of Mexico's national resources: gold is a skeleton — opposite is iron in forged blocks — silver is a knife — oil spurts forth from the teeth of the skull. The

last panel is entitled **Proletarian Struggle.** It shows a world without order without justice: men fight and kill each other: chaos.

Supreme Court of Justice, Mexico City, 1941:
top, **Justice,** general view; detail of **Justice;**
detail of **False Justice** and bottom, **Proletarian Struggle**

99

Immediately after the completion of the Supreme Court cycle, Orozco started work on the vaults of the Church of the Hospital of Jesus just a few blocks away. One of the oldest buildings in Mexico City, it was reputed to hold Cortez's last remains and was an important national monument. The title of Orozco's murals was **An Allegory of the Apocalypse in Relation to Modern Times** and while it was intended that he should cover the whole of the walls and vaults, funds for this were not made available and only the West wall and the two west vaults of the nave were ever completed. Orozco worked on the church from 1942 to 1944 and at the same time also worked on a number of easel paintings with religious themes (cat.194-196). Orozco's attitude to religion was, as ever, equivocal, the ideals of christianity were, as with all ideologies, too easily perverted by those very institutions which were founded to serve them. The image of the outraged Christ destroying his cross had special significance for Orozco and was to recur throughout his work. This work in its unfinished form divides into two halves; the dominant colours of the first half are cool: sombre greens, greys and blacks suggesting tragedy and death. Four Evangelists surround a Godhead — a jagged and violent force bearing a likeness to the ancient Aztec glyph for 'the destruction of a city'. Below on either side of a window are separate figures of male and female mourners sitting before open graves. On the vault above

them is the image of a figure being torn apart — it is Evil wracked by the upholders of truth, who with other contorted figures suffers the agonies of the Last Judgement. The second vault is in marked contrast — its colour range is warm reds, greys and blacks. Four apocalyptic beasts extend over the vault — three horses and a jaguar — astride the jaguar, a symbol of Mexico which previously appeared in **The Jiquilpan Allegory** and **National Wealth —** is the whore of Babylon.

Whore of Babylon, 1942-44

The 1940s were a period of huge output for Orozco, yet there is some indication that he was compelled to create new forms by the feeling that his previous work had somehow become devalued or lost its force. He was obviously talking about his own work when in 1947 he wrote about the history of the Mexican mural movement.

'**. . . there is the trend of revolutionary socialist propaganda, in which there continues to appear with surprising persistency, Christian iconography . . . [this is] superficially modernised; perhaps rifles and machine guns in place of bows and arrows; aeroplanes instead of angels; flying atomic bombs in place of divine damnation; and a confused and fantastic paradise in a future very difficult to define. To all this out-dated religious imagery very nineteenth-century liberal symbols are added. Freedom with its Phrygian cap and the indispensable broken chains; democracy; peace; blindfolded justice; the Nation . . . Very ancient symbols of the "Bourgeoisie, enemy of progress" type still play a prominent part in murals represented by pot-bellied toffs in top hats or by pigs, jackals, dragons or other monsters; so well known and so familiar that they are as inoffensive as the plumed serpent.'**

In his search for new forms Orozco began to work increasingly on a smaller scale. During the '40s he made many drawings and easel paintings — portraiture became a major source of income — and from 1941 to 1946, looking back to the themes of his earliest work, he made many tempera studies and drawings of popular life in the slums and bar rooms (cat.77-108). In 1944 he

Female Mourner
Church of the Hospital of Jesus, Mexico City, 1942-44

began to make his first etchings and continued to experiment in this medium (cat. 85, 87-92). He also started, round about this time, a series of oil paintings based on anti-military and anti-clerical subjects: the despot and the dictator were ridiculed in works with such titles as **Perfume and Pomade, Demagogue, The Tyrant** and **Small Nation;** these are in essence painted caricatures (cat.139,141,142,134).

Perfume and Pomade
oil on canvas, 1946
(cat.139)

At this time Orozco began to work on a series of drawings on a set theme. The first of these, made in 1945, was called **Truth** (cat.151-163) and the whole series comprised an exhibition at the newly founded Colegio Nacional. Subsequent series were entitled **Demagogy** (1948) and **Conservative Oppression** (1948) (cat.164,165; 166-170).

Procession, 1948
charcoal and crayon from series
Conservative Oppression
(cat.167)

In 1947, he was given a major retrospective exhibition in the Palacio de Bellas Artes and also made a smaller exhibition entitled **Los Teules** — The White Gods — at the Colegio Nacional (cat.179-189). **Los Teules** referred to the names the Indians gave to the Spanish conquerors: it was part of their belief that Quetzalcoatl (the White God) would one day return. This did, in fact, happen and the Spaniard brought with him his own white gods. Painted either in tempera or piroxiline, these works brought alive the dislocated Indian past — the skull, the mask, the dismembered body. Sombre images of barbarity and cruelty. The coarseness and violence is disquieting — it is outside the sphere of mortality and bypasses human sympathy. It is a primordial statement of man's power to destroy.

This work seemed depressing and without hope and, after completing this series, Orozco embarked on one of the most important of his later murals: **National Allegory** in the open air theatre in the National School for Teachers, Mexico City. This was the first open air mural in Mexico, painted in ethyl silicate, a new medium, on a concrete parabolic wall, six stories in height, flanked on either side by classroom wings. Orozco described it:

'A National Allegory, in large geometric shapes (stone-like and metallic). In the centre, the eagle and serpent, representing life and death: the symbol of Mexico. On the left, a man with his head in the clouds ascends an enormous ladder, on the right a hand polishes stone.'

National Allegory
outdoor mural, National School for Teachers
Mexico City, 1947-48
reproduced in colour on p.93

The man, whose head cannot be seen, suggests aspiration, beside him mount spirals: chemical apparatus or the smoke and flames of revolutionary struggle? Iron beams in exaggerated perspective shoot out from the surface of the wall. On the right of the mural are more ordered forms; they suggest the rational — a laboratory or a factory. These are, perhaps, the future of Mexico. In this mural, abstract forms have been used symbolically with colour to retain a sympathy with the surrounding buildings, and to construct a 'poem' about Mexico; the overliteral nature of the two previous allegories (in Jiquilpan and the Law Courts) has been transcended. During the mid 1940s Orozco had first begun to look into the possibilities of abstraction — this was a natural consequence of his experiment with the **Dive Bomber**. And during his stay in New York in 1945 he had further experimented in a number of semi-abstract easel paintings. In 1949, the year of his death, he was planning to carry on from **National Allegory** in another outdoor mural using abstract geometrical forms. This was to be situated in an intensive housing development in Mexico City (cat.298, 299).

But Orozco also continued to work on more conventional commissions. In 1948 he worked on two murals, both treating the historical development of the Mexican Republic. The first, entitled **Benito Juárez, the Church and the Imperialists** was situated in the Sala de Reforma in Chapultepec Castle, a national monument which looks out over Mexico City. Four metres high by six and a half metres long, the mural is dominated by the large indian head of Benito Juárez (1806-72), President of the Republic and vanquisher of Louis Napoleon's puppet Emperor: Maximilian. Juárez's head, like an icon, rises triumphant over the vanquished forces of Imperialism and the Church, but the subject did not really allow great scope for Orozco's imagination and some of the images are reworkings from earlier themes. More impressive is the mural **Hidalgo and the Great Mexican Revolutionary Legislation** which Orozco began during the winter of 1948-49 on the vault of the Chamber of Deputies of the state of Jalisco. This was situated in the Government Palace in Guadalajara, just a few yards away from his earlier depiction of Hidalgo on the main staircase. The subjects of the mural were Hidalgo's decree abolishing slavery in Mexico, the first of its kind in the American continent, the agrarian laws of Morelos and the Reform Laws and Constitutions of 1857 and 1917. Desmond Rochfort has already written of the contrast between the messianic Hidalgo on the staircase and the depiction here; this reflects clearly the changes in Orozco's attitudes during the intervening ten years. Hidalgo is now tentative, almost frightened. He is freeing the slaves who, bound and contorted by ropes, chains and barbed wire, thrust their anguished bodies towards him. Hidalgo's apprehensiveness is perhaps explained by Orozco's knowledge of Mexican (and world) history. Yes, the slaves were free, but for what? Freed to kill and be killed, free to continue to be exploited, free to die free? Orozco was of course referring not only to the historical fact of the abolition of slavery but also to the present. The figures of slaves occur in his drawings and easel paintings during that year (cat.171-178); they are a testament to corruption, exploitation and dictatorship.

The work of Orozco's last few years seems devoid of hope — what *is* the humanitarian response to continuing genocide, atomic destruction and corruption? The worm-eaten galleon of world history was manned by self-seekers — idiots and fools. Orozco was getting older — he was 66 — he had suffered intermittent trouble with his heart — and hope — although not energy — was running out. In a late painting (cat.203) made some time in 1948, Orozco made what was, perhaps, some kind of final statement. The title is **Metaphysical Landscape** but the format is as in a portrait; from the top edge of the painting, a black thickly painted shape descends over a striated, grey, receding horizon. On 7 September 1949, without warning, Orozco's heart stopped beating.

Metaphysical Painting
piroxiline on masonite, 1948
(cat.203)
illustrated in colour on p.96

Mask with Butterfly
piroxiline on masonite, from series **Los Teules** (White Gods), 1947
(cat.186)

Dive Bomber and Tank, 1940

Fresco 9 × 18ft on six panels 9 × 3ft each
Collection: The Museum of Modern Art, New York
Commissioned through the Abbey Aldrich Rockefeller Fund

Orozco 'Explains'

This 'explanation' was written by Mr. Orozco. The quotation marks in his title indicate his feeling that explanations are unnecessary.

Published in *The Bulletin of the Museum of Modern Art.* 4. Vol.vii. August 1940.

● The public wants explanations about a painting. What the artist had in mind when he did it. What he was thinking of. What is the exact name of the picture, and what the artist means by that. If he is glorifying or cursing. If he believes in democracy.

Going to the Italian Opera you get a booklet with a full account of why Rigoletto kills Aïda at the end of a wild party with La Bohème, Lucia di Lammermoor and Madame Butterfly.

The Italian Renaissance is another marvelous opera full of killings and wild parties, and the

public gets also thousands of booklets with complete and most detailed information about everything and everybody in Florence and Rome.

And now the public insists on knowing the plot

of modern painted opera, though not italian, of course. They take for granted that every picture must be the illustration of a short story or of a thesis and want to be told the entertaining biography and bright sayings of the leaders in the stage-picture, the ups and downs of hero, villain, and chorus. Many pictures actually tell all that and more even including quotations from the Holy Scriptures and Shakespeare. Others deal with social conditions, evils of the world, revolutions, history and the like. Bedroom pictures with *la femme à sa toilette* are still very frequent.

Suddenly, Madam Butterfly and her friend Rigoletto disappear from the stage-picture. Gone, too, are gloomy social conditions. To the amazement of the public the curtain goes up and nothing is on the stage but a few lines and cubes. The abstract. The public protests and demands explanations, and explanations are given away freely and generously. Rigoletto and social conditions are still there but have become

abstract, all dolled up in cubes and cones in a wild surrealist party with La Bohème, Lucia di Lammermoor and Madame Butterfly. Meanings? Names? Significance? Short stories? Well, let's invent them afterwards. The public refuses TO SEE painting. They want TO HEAR painting. They don't care for the show itself, they prefer TO LISTEN to the barker outside. Free lectures every hour for the blind, around the museum. This way, please.

'The Artist must be sincere', they say. It is true. He must be sincere. The actor on the stage commits suicide to thrill or frighten the public to death. The actor feels exactly what a suicide feels, and acts the same way except that his gun is not loaded. He is sincere as an artist only. Next week he has to impersonate St. Francis, Lenin or an average business man, very sincerely!

The technique of painting is still in its infancy after ten thousand years of civilization, or

whatever it is. Even college children know this fact, for abundant literature about the subject is on hand.

It seems incredible that science and industry have not yet provided the artist with better materials to work with. Not a single improvement through centuries. The range of colors available is still extremely limited. Pigments are not permanent at all in spite of manufacturers' claims. Canvas, wood, paper, walls are exposed to continuous destruction from moisture, changes in temperature, chemical reactions, insects and germs. Oils, varnishes, wax, gums and tempera media are dirty substances darkening, changing, crackling and disintegrating all the time.

Fresco painting is free from the inconvenience of oils and varnishes, but the wall upon which the painting is done is subjected to many causes of destruction, such as the use of the wrong kind of building materials, poor planning, moisture from the ground or from the air, earthquakes, dive bombing, tanking or battleshipping, excess of

'The Dive Bomber', or six interchangeable panels

A painting is a *poem* and nothing else. A poem made of relationships between words, sounds or ideas. Sculpture and architecture are also relationships between forms. This word *forms* includes color, tone, proportion, line, et cetera.

The forms in a poem are necessarily organized in such a way that the whole acts as an automatic machine, more or less efficient but apt to function in a certain way, to move in a certain direction. Such a machine-motor sets in motion our senses, first; our emotional capacity, second; and our intellect, last. An efficient and well-organized machine may work in very different ways. It can be simplified to its last elemental or basic structure or may be developed into a vast and complicated organism working under the same basic principles.

Each part of a machine may be by itself a machine to function independently from the whole. The order of the inter-relations between its parts may be altered, but those relationships may stay the same in any other order, and unexpected or expected possibilities may appear. Suppose we change the actual order of the plastic elements of the vaults in the Sistine Chapel . . .

A linotype is a work of art, but a linotype in motion is an extraordinary adventure affecting the lives of many human beings or the course of history. A few lines from a linotype in action may start a world war or may mean the birth of a new era.

magnesia in the lime or the marble dust, lack of care resulting in scratches or peeling off, et cetera. So, fresco must be done only on walls that are as free as possible from all these inconveniences.

There is no rule for painting al fresco. Every artist may do as he pleases provided he paints as thinly as possible and only while the plaster is wet, six to eight hours from the moment it is applied. No retouching of any kind afterwards. Every artist develops his own way of planning his conception and transferring it onto the wet plaster. Every method is as good as the other. Or the artist may improvise without any previous sketches.

Note:

[1] Moveable panels (each 9 by 3 feet) are made with strong steel frames. The plaster is held by a wire mesh. Panels such as these are too heavy to be really movable without danger to the painting. That is a field where technology may be of great service to art by developing a process for the construction of special panels for fresco painting. They must be very light in weight and at the same time so absorbent as to slow the drying as much as possible. In addition, the plaster for these panels must be less brittle than the ordinary one, probably by adding some new

material to the plaster or by any other way to turn it very hard and flexible and as absorbent as before.

[2] Plaster is the same as for regular walls: lime and sand or lime and marble dust. A very small amount of Portland cement may be added if necessary to make a harder material, in certain cases. It is better to avoid it. For the intonaco or final coat upon which the painting is done no cement is used. Proportions: 2 parts sand to 1 lime or 2 to 1½. The number of coats of plaster must be as many as possible to hold a great deal of moisture. The number of coats of

plaster must be as many as possible to hold a great deal of moisture. The number of coats depends upon the kind of material the wall is made of. The best material is the old hand-made brick because modern machine-made brick is as waterproof as concrete.

[3] Only limeproof colors are used such as: earthen colors, Mars colors, cobalt, chromium oxide, non-animal blacks and lime white. Good cadmiums may be used also very thinly. The binding medium is the carbonate of lime produced during the drying process of plaster. A fresco is never varnished.

Juárez, the Church and the Imperialists
Mural in
The Sala de Reforma, Chapultepec Castle,
Mexico City, 1948

Total area 26 sq. metres

Benito Juárez (1806-72) became President of Mexico in 1861 as leader of the divided Liberals. He put forward a strong anti-clerical policy as he felt that the power of the Church both impeded progress and looked back to the days of Spanish domination. He was pressed by the European powers for the repayment of large and long-outstanding debts. He foreclosed on these debts and this led to military action in 1864. Louis Napoleon sent troops who set up the Austrian, Maximilian as Emperor of Mexico. He was welcomed by the monarchists and dispossessed clergy. The Western powers and Maximilian are shown in the lower part of the mural.

In 1867 Juárez and the Republican forces rallied and deposed the Emperor. On June 19 Maximilian was executed.

THE WASHINGTON POST
Sunday, August 29, 1948

Compared With Rivera's

On Power of Orozco's 'Juarez'

This is the Chapultepec "Juarez" mural of Jose Celments Orozco

By Jane Watson Crane

PORTRAITS OF THE Mexican Indian, Benito Juarez, Nineteenth Century leader of the famous reform movement and twice President, are featured in murals completed this year in Mexico City by both Orozco and Rivera. The Rivera mural, executed for the dining room of the new Hotel Prado, has been widely publicized as a sensation in the United States, mainly because of the antireligious character of its message. The Orozco, superior in painting and conception, has gone virtually unnoticed. The latter, a fresco mounted on a steel screen and measuring about 14 by 20 feet, is in the National Museum of History in Chapultepec Castle, the historic fortress which came to the fore once again as the setting for the 1945 Inter-American Conference.

Orozco's 1948 fresco combines elements of his earlier and later work. The disembodied head of Juarez, heroic in size, is surrounded by smaller half-figures and heads relating to the struggle between liberals and conservatives, set off by the law attacking special privilege. The familiar flaming torch, the banner, the raised swords, and the bowed heads appear in this composition. There is also the head of a monster, not unlike the medieval gargoyles seen on French churches, and an elongated human body with a 'death's head.

Compared to the design and movement of the Orozco, the Rivera appears static and poster-like. With Rivera it is the story-telling approach, with Orozco it is "design and the idea."

The Rivera has already appeared in reproduction in United States newspapers and magazines. There is a full-page reproduction of the Orozco in the August issue of Panorama, issued by the department of cultural affairs of the Pan American Union.

A. U. Act to Be Shown

EIGHT ARTISTS on the faculty of American University art honored with a special sh the Union beginning Sep to circulate the group opening here. The e program of collabor

institutions and the division of cultural affairs, will continue on view throughout the month.

Artists represented are William Calfee, head of the department; Sarah Baker, Robert Gates, Pietro Lazzari, Leo Steppat, Joe Summerford, John Galloway, and Jack Tworkov. Galloway, who is also editor of the university's art publication, Right Angle, painted the 1948 Pan American Day poster for the Union.

Latin American Art Guide

LONG IN PROCESS of completion, the Library of Congress has finally published "A Guide to the Art of Latin America," an invaluable compendium of bibliographical data, providing, so far as we know, the only organized basis for study in this field in the U.S.A. The editing of this useful tome was done by Robert C. Smith and Elizabeth Wilder, formerly of the staff of the Hispanic Founda in the Library of Congress. They were ai a group of advisory editors, mainly of Latin ica. Mario Buschiazzo of Buenos Aires store of bibliographical knowledge at t posal. Jean Richmond, of Smith Colle Library of Congress, did the job of pr manuscript for the press. The pape No. 21 in the Library's Latin contains close to 500 printe

Two notes of warning may be misleading to so bibliographical guide, an not go beyond 1942. search should be m art sections of t' Studies," the c lection of th other scatt through publicat

Rare except gen

**Hidalgo:
The Great Mexican
Revolutionary
Legislation
and the Abolition
of Slavery:
Mural in the Chamber
of Deputies, Palace
of Government,
Guadalajara,
1948-49**

Total area 200 sq. metres

Detail from above left

Head with Key, charcoal and crayon, 1948 (cat.168)

The Slave, prioxiline on masonite, 1948 (cat.178)

J.C. Orozco

Notes concerning the Technique of Mural Painting in Mexico during the Last Twenty-Five Years

A text prepared for the catalogue of
his retrospective exhibition held in 1947
in the Palacio de Bellas Artes,
Mexico City

fresco: a kind of painting executed
in watercolour on mortar or
plaster which is not quite dry.

● In 1921 Mexican painters were called to cover large mural surfaces of public buildings and, not having previous knowledge of the technique for this work, they began researching and carrying out experiments. The first thing that occurred to them was to look at the ancient classical methods, which had been almost forgotten. They rejected out of hand the use of oil paint, as this is totally inappropriate for mural painting for a great number of reasons, among which were the disastrous experiences of painters in earlier centuries.

Some of the new muralists began to work with resins, essences and beeswax (both hot and cold). However, they soon discarded these as they decomposed easily, were very dirty, and gave very similar results to oil paint.

Immediately experimentation began with the method called FRESCO, the most ancient in the history of human culture, the most resistant to date, and that which has preserved for us the sensitivity and thought of pre-Hispanic man. In the numerous caves of the Quaternary era (still in the process of exploration), in Spain and France, and possibly in almost all parts of the earth, one can see the first works of mural painting. Obviously, these were done over panels which were still 'fresh' (fresco), perhaps of very hard clay, perhaps of some mixture of lime materials, or simply over very absorbent rock, also of lime. If the Paleolithic and Neolithic painters used other means to secure their paintings to the rocks we do not know of them: perhaps they used an animal or vegetable fat or the sap of a tree or herb, although this is doubtful. The sketches are too precise to have been done with oily materials. It is also hard to believe that an animal or vegetable fat could have remained in good condition for 10, 15, 20 or 30 thousand years. The paleolithic paintings are, necessarily, FRESCOES.

After a long period of study which had started in 1908, I began my first attempts at fresco mural paintings on the walls of the large courtyard at the National Preparatory School (the old College of San Ildefonso) in 1923. I was immediately confronted with a series of exciting problems to resolve:

'How to give a concrete form to my ideas?'
'Whether to make scale drawings of the compositions on paper like an architect — or

whether to work directly on the wall?'
'What relationship should there be between the paintings and the real space of the building where they interact?'
'How to prepare the walls to receive the level plaster? What materials to use in this?'
'How to transfer the drawing onto the fresco surface?'
'What colours and brushes to use?'
'How to continue the work without damaging the work of the previous days?'
'How to make corrections?'

The knowledge of my new trade was derived from four sources: First: the treatise on painting written by Cennino Cennini. Second: the elemental, but very valuable experience of the Mexican stonemasons. Third: the detailed study of some very old Mexican frescoes, pre-Cortesian and colonial. Fourth: my own daily and direct experience on the walls of the Preparatory School. I carried out many tests to try to discover the reasons for the successes and incidental failures.

It is well-known that the book written by Cennino Cennini (the 15th-century painter and the son of a pupil of a pupil of Giotto), is the only complete, perfectly clear and concise treatise on painting that has been left to us from the past. It is also the only one which gives an exact account of the methods used by all the great European painters of the 14th, 15th and 16th centuries, direct inheritors of Greek traditions. Cennini shows us, in the clearest language possible and in great detail how to paint walls by fresco.

I at once had at my disposal the knowledge of a humble bricklayer, who placed himself at my service. Such men do not know about many different things, but what they do know is of great value.

The study of the ancient Mexican frescos, many of which are in magnificent condition, taught me a great deal, especially with regard to the reasons for deterioration and destruction.

Finally, for my part, the most valuable of all has been my own daily and direct experience.

This sort of fresco method is simple and suitable to the type of construction materials which have been used until now in the building of human habitations, in which it is extremely difficult, if not impossible, to vary the method in

113

any fundamental way. If bricks, stones, lime and sand are used in the construction of the walls, fresco can be used. The bricks and stones can be substituted for modern steel frames, but the lime and sand (or the marble dust) must be left. The walls may be of concrete, but they must also have a lime coating. It is for this reason that the modifications, or perfections, which contemporary painters have introduced refer only to the methods of execution or to modern techniques for conservation of the painted area which can be carried out before it sets. One of the most important modifications which I felt compelled to introduce was the following: the ancient fresco painters did not make preliminary drawings of their compositions; at most they made sketches or took notes of important details, like busts or heads. The pen drawings of the High Renaissance painters are well known. From the beginning the Hellenic frescoists used (and still use) stencils, i.e. paper cardboard models, called 'antivola', to make an infinite number of figures of Christs, saints or apostles.

The composition was drawn directly in red onto the roughly prepared wall. The main divisions were marked by simple lines. This drawing was then covered, fragment by fragment, from top to bottom with a fine layer of the mixture with which the painting was to be painted.

Work in progress on **The Departure of Quetzalcoatl**, Dartmouth College, 1932-34

This method is good for panels of a modest size, but when worked on large surfaces (especially vaults or domes), it does not allow the painting to be freely executed. I have found it in this case preferable to make a scale drawing as does an architect when he is planning the construction of a building or a topographer when he is drawing a map. The method is the following: make a number of drawings to scale, taking into account all the conditions of space, size and light, not only

of the mural, but also of the architecture around where it is to be placed. Once a final choice has been made, transfer the basic geometric outline to the vault or dome (but only the general outline which determines the outer limits of the composition). Within this geometric structure the principal points of the minor divisions are discovered by means of rectangular coordinates, using as axes the nearest perpendiculars. This operation can be done in a few minutes over the fresh panel. In this way precise and invariable points and lines can be discerned. Over this the figures can then be freely constructed, knowing with certainty, in centimetres, the range of modifications possible at any moment, whilst full control is maintained over the whole composition. This enables the painter to organise live shapes freely within a controlled and precise network. In cases where it is impossible to see the progress of the painting at a distance (because of scaffolding) this method is extraordinarily efficient in judging at a short distance the effect of what is appearing; this is usually the case when painting vaults and domes.

There are three methods of painting, any of these can be used: by transparency, by opacity or by a combination of both.

In fresco painting, light tones can be obtained, as in watercolour, by using less pigment and adding water, which makes the bright white of the panel show through. But light tones can also be made by mixing colours with the white pigment (in this case lime carbonate), which is very opaque.

The Renaissance frescoists preferred the first method; the rest of the ancient fresco painters used the second. The final effect of the two methods are very different, but both are equally rich and powerful.

Since my first attempts at fresco painting I

have used both methods. Another resource which is very peculiar to the fresco is colouring the mixture itself by mixing in a large quantity of pigment before applying to the wall (on small or large surfaces). Transparent or opaque colours can still be painted over this layer, provided that the wall contains a large quantity of water and that it dries very slowly.

● Wall Preparation

The preparation of walls or vaults which are to be painted in fresco varies enormously, depending on the materials with which they have been built, the condition they are in, and the sort of deterioration that affects them.

A large number of buildings where Mexican painters have had the opportunity to paint are of the colonial type, which are very solid and well-built. The materials are the same as those used in Mexico 30 years ago, before the introduction of concrete and metal structures: hewn stone, 'recinto', volcanic rock, brick, and dressed stone. Construction rock is not found in important buildings.

The first thing to do is to strip off all the old panels, generally in very bad condition, leaving the foundation material bare. Wash this immediately with clean water to remove all the saltpetre possible. In the National Preparatory School I used a large quantity of potassium cyanide dissolved in water to destroy the microscopic vegetation which the salts (known by the name of saltpetre) produce. This cyanide water is used to wash the walls and the sand for the mixture.

After washing the wall, fill in all the cracks with new material, and put as many layers of thick mixture (and small pieces of brick) as are needed to obtain an even surface and a degree of thickness capable of containing large quantities of water, very necessary for a perfect setting and colour fastness. These layers of thick mixture are not applied vertically, but following the shape of the wall.

The same method is used in the preparation of vaults or domes. The only difference is that it must be done with a high pressure water hose.

The colonial buildings where I have had the opportunity to paint are the following: The National Preparatory School, The Casa de los Azulejos (Sanborn's) and the Temple of Jesus, all in Mexico City; the Hospicio Cabañas and the Palace of Government in Guadalajara.

In this latter city very good quality sand and lime can be found, which, when set, produces a very hard mixture. The sand is yellow and contains a clay which the bricklayers call 'putty'. It is this which gives the mixture its hardness. Some months later one has to use a chisel and much effort to break up a level piece. This is also a yellowish colour and contrasts admirably with the white (lime carbonate) of the painting.

Modern buildings are concrete, a material which is not very absorbent. An ordinary mortar of lime and sand does not adhere to it easily.

In Pomona College, California, all that was available was a concrete wall, which had been covered with a very delicate layer of lime and porous material. This was put there for 'acoustic purposes' to stop the echo, and was probably made with pumice stone. Over this material I directly spread the mixture (made of lime and fine sand of very good quality), without much hope that it would adhere well, but until the present day it is still in good condition. It has already lasted 16 years.

A few years later, Diego Rivera faced a similar problem with the concrete walls in Detroit. He and his engineer friends came up with another solution: they constructed steel frames covered with wire and metal sheets, capable of firmly sustaining a layer of cement, lime and sand or marble dust over which the fresco could be painted. The total thickness of this layer is about three centimetres.

I myself have painted over these frames in the Palace of Fine Art, in the new building of the Supreme Court of Justice in Mexico City and also in the Museum of Modern Art in New York. In the Supreme Court I was helped by Rivera's able assistant Andres Sanchez Flores, who has specialised in this type of work.

Orozco working on steel-framed panels at the Museum of Modern Art, New York, 1940

The first layer, which goes into the interstices (without the wire and metal sheets), is made of white cement, thick marble dust and lime in equal parts. The reason for using cement is to stop the metal expanding and breaking the panel, as it has almost the same coefficient of expansion as steel. Then three or four layers are laid on. These consist of two parts marble dust, and lime in equal parts is then applied.

The frame is solidly fixed to the wall with bolts and brackets, but a space of some 10 or 15 centimetres is left between the two. The advantages of this procedure are very important: the painting is kept almost completely separate from the wall and its weaknesses. Dampness does not reach it, and if the panel is well built, it will remain in good condition for an indefinite length of time.

The disadvantages are: on very large surfaces, such as vaults and domes, metallic panels could prove to be too heavy for the construction and are also too costly. This is only a relative disadvantage. The really serious thing is that it is not a direct painting which forms part of the architectonic construction itself. It is artificial, a type of mask or dress, which, because of its independence, loses much of its own organic function. Moreover, the thinness of the panel does not allow for a deep type of treatment as in a proper wall.

However, if the building is planned to be decorated from the beginning (whatever places have been selected for fresco painting), more solid panels can be built. Panels, moreover, which would be more harmonious with the general structure of the building, the same as windows or staircases and not merely as occasional additions.

● **The Ideas**

Having studied the themes in modern Mexican mural paintings, we find the following facts: all the painters began with subjects derived from traditional iconography, either Christian or Frankish, and often literally copied them.

In the first murals we find the bearded or beardless figure of the Pantocrator, virgins, angels, saint-burials, martyrs and even the Virgin of Guadalupe. All that was missing was the Sacred Heart of Jesus and Saint Anthony.

After the first period three perfectly definable trends appeared: the Indian trend in its two variants: the archaic and the colourfully folkloric — the Olympian, Toltec or Aztec and the types and traditions of the present Indian artists with all their magnificent richness of colour.

The second trend has an historical content in which Mexican history, preferably the Conquest, is dealt with; history is shown from contradictory and opposing viewpoints. Those who are heroes in one mural are villains in another.

Ancient Mexican Religion
lunette from Hospicio Cabañas, Guadalajara, 1938-39

And lastly, there is the trend of revolutionary socialist propaganda, in which there continues to appear, with surprising persistency, Christian iconography. Its interminable martyrs, persecutions, miracles, prophets, saint-fathers, evangelists, supreme pontiffs, final judgements, hells and heavens, the just and sinners, heretics, schismatics, triumphs of the Church, Byzantine discussions, iconoclastic emperors, Councils, Savonarolas, inquisitors, Jesuits, Hope and Charity, the Saintly Sepulchre, and even the Crusades. All these are superficially modernised; perhaps rifles and machine-guns in place of bows and arrows; aeroplanes instead of angels; flying atomic bombs in place of divine damnation and a confused and fantastic paradise in a future very difficult to define.

Detail from **False Justice**
mural in Supreme Court of Justice, Mexico City, 1941

To all this outdated religious imagery very 19th century liberal symbols are added. Freedom with its Phrygian cap and the indispensable broken chains; Democracy; Peace; Blindfolded Justice carrying its sword and scales; The Nation; torches, stars, palms, olives and nopals; heraldic or symbolic animals, including eagles, lions, tigers, horses and serpents. Very ancient symbols of the 'Bourgeoisie, enemy of progress' type, still play a prominent part in murals, represented by pot-bellied toffs in top hats, or by pigs, jackals, dragons or other monsters, so well-known and familiar that they are as inoffensive as the plumed serpent.

Catalogue

The works in this list have been loosely grouped under separate headings which will reflect their appearance within **the sequence of the exhibition**. The groups were selected on the basis of genre or subject matter and, taken together, they not only indicate the wide range of Orozco's interests but also the chronological development of his work. **Studies for murals** have been separated from the main sequence.

The convention of the group is one of convenience: it breaks up and gives form to a long numerical sequence. Some of the groups could overlap and the inclusion of a work under one heading rather than another has in some cases been on a fine point of judgement.

Titles are given in English, wherever there has been an idiomatic translation the Spanish title is given in brackets.

Measurements are given in centimetres, height preceding width. Works are on paper where no support is specified.

Although loans have come from many sources a large number have come from the collections listed below. These are represented in the listing by the abbreviations as marked:
INBA: Instituto Nacional de Bellas Artes, Mexico DF (National Institute of Fine Arts, Mexico City)
CG: INBA, Museo de Arte Carillo Gil, Mexico DF (The Carillo Gil Art Museum, Mexico City)
OF: Collection of the Orozco family, Mexico
All other lenders are credited in full.

Paintings and Graphics

'The House of Tears'
Brothel scenes
Young Girls
and Popular Subjects,
1910-15

1. **The Cinema** 1910-13
    Pencil / 34×52.6 / CG
2. **Young Girl** 1910-13
    Pencil / 18×12.5 / CG
3. **The Little Darling (La Chole)**
    Pencil / 41.5×21.5 / CG
4. **The Blue Bed** 1912
    Watercolour / 33.5×50 / CG
5. **The Desperate Woman** 1912
    Watercolour / 33.5×50.5 / CG
6. **The Dance of the Pickpockets No.1 (Baile de Pepenches)** 1912-13
    Watercolour / 22×31.3 / CG
7. **Dance of the Pickpockets No.2** 1913
    Pencil & wash / 15.2×22.5 / CG
8. **The Hour of the Gigolo (La Hora del Chulo)** 1913
    Watercolour / 28×45.5 / CG
9. **Prostitutes' Games (Juego de Prostitutas)** 1913
    Watercolour / 44×60
    Coll: Ing. & Sra J. Espinosa Ulloa
10. **The Meeting** 1913
    Watercolour / 33.5×32 / CG
11. **Bedroom** 1913
    Watercolour / 53×59 / OF

12. **The Room** 1913
    Watercolour / 39×53
    Coll: Ing. & Sra J. Espinosa Ulloa
13. **Driftwood** 1915
    Oil on canvas / 50.5×60 / CG
14. **The Curtain of Sorrow** n.d.
    Watercolour / 30×50 /
    Private coll. Mexico City

Scenes from
the Revolution:
A number of these
have been dated as early
as 1913-17 but on documentary
and stylistic evidence it is
likely that they were not
started before 1926

15. **Plunder**
    Wash / 20×27 / CG
16. **La Cucaracha No.1**
    Ink / 31×48 / CG
    The *cucaracha* (cockroach) is a popular Mexican dance
17. **La Cucaracha No.3**
    Ink / 30.2×43 / CG
18. **Aristrocratic Dance**
    1913-17
    Wash / 30.5×45 / CG
19. **Wounded**
    Wash / 30.9×47 / CG
20. **The Reactionary**
    Wash / 32×48 / CG
21. **The Field of Battle**
    Wash / 18×31 / CG
22. **Combat** 1920
    Oil on canvas / 66.5×88 / CG
23 **The White House**
    Oil on canvas / 62×76 / CG
24 **The Dead Man**
    Oil on canvas / 55×60 / CG
25 **The Dead Boy**
    Oil on canvas / 4×51 / CG
26. **Little Girl with Sombrero** Ink / 25.3×24 / INBA
27. **The Battle** 1925
    Ink / 32×49 / CG
28. **Common Grave**
    Ink / 29.8×47 / CG
29. **The Major-Domo**
    Ink / 30×41.5 / CG
30. **The Explosion**
    Ink / 29.8×47 / CG
31. **The Hanged Man** 1925
    Ink / 41.5×31 / CG
32. **The Camp Followers** 1926 **(Las Soldaderas)**
    Oil on canvas / 80×95 / INBA, Museo de Arte Moderno, Mexico City
    This image is strongly linked to the National Preparatory School Mural **Return to the Battlefield** 1926 as well as to cat.39 **The Rear Guard** 1929 and a large number of drawings.
33. **The Shot Man** 1928
    Ink / 35.2×48 / CG
34. **The Requiem** 1928
    Ink / 32×43 / CG

35. **War** 1928
    Ink / 32×43 / CG
36. **'In the Hills'** 1928
    Ink / 33×49 / CG
37. **The Flag** 1928
    Litho / 26.5×42.4 / CG
38. **Mexican Soldiers** 1929
    Litho / 28.3×45.3 / CG
39. **The Rear Guard** 1929
    Litho / 35.4×47.3 / CG
40. **Ruined House** 1929
    Litho / 32.6×45.8 / CG
41. **The Maguey** 1929
    Litho / 25×40.5 / CG
42. **Little Indians** 1929
    Litho / 31×43.3 / CG

Cat.39, 43-49 are all based on subjects from the National Preparatory School murals

43. **Hands** 1930
    Litho / 42.6×22.9 / CG
44. **The Friar and the Indian** 1930
    Litho / 31.5×26.5 / CG
45. **The Pregnant Woman** 1930
    Litho / 40.4×25.4 / CG
46. **The Pregnant Woman** 1930
    Litho / 40.4×25.4 / CG
47. **Affliction** 1930
    Litho / 30×25.2 / CG
48. **Three Generations** 1930
    Litho / 26.5×37.6 / CG
49. **Head of a Peasant Woman** 1930
    Litho / 35.4×25.2 / CG
50. **Mexican People** 1930
    Litho / 27.6×38.9 / CG
51. **Mexican Landscape** 1930
    Litho / 31.8×43.8 / CG
52. **Mexican Hills** 1930
    Oil on canvas / 42×59.5 / CG
53. **Zapata** 1930
    Oil on canvas / 37×23 / CG
54. **Parade of Zapatistas** 1930
    Gouache / 37×56.5 / CG
    Sketch for cat.no.55
55. **Parade of Zapatistas** 1931
    Oil and tempera on canvas / 65×97
    Coll: Lic. G. Martínez Domínguez, Mexico City. A version of this work is also in the collection of the Museum of Modern Art in New York
56. **The Maguey** 1932
    Oil on canvas / 71.5×92 / Museo Nacional de Bellas Artes, Havana, Cuba

North American
Scenes

57. **The El** 1930
    Oil on canvas / 75×57.5 / CG
58. **The Dead** 1931
    Oil on canvas / 110×92 / CG
59. **Winter 1932**
    Oil on canvas / 38×46.5 / CG
60. **Queensborough Bridge** 1932
    Oil on canvas / 54.5×70 / CG

61. **Three Heads** 1932
Oil on canvas / 47×38.5 / CG

**Prints from the
Mexican Suite, 1935**

62. **Tourists and Aztecs**
Litho / 30.5×41.3 / CG
63. **Rocky Ground**
Litho / 32.6×41.6 / CG
64. **Demonstration**
Litho / 33.5×42.9 / CG
65. **The Masses**
Litho / 33.7×42.9 / CG
Related to a panel in the Jiquilpan
murals, 1940

Portraits

66. **Senora Eva Sikelianos** 1928
Oil on canvas / 56.5×56 / CG
67. **Julia Peterkin** 1930
Oil on canvas / 53×38 / CG
68. **Luis Cardoza y Aragón**
Tempera on canvas / 55×44
Private collection, Mexico City
69. **María Luisa Lacy** 1942
Oil on canvas / 59×66.5 / Coll:
Ing. & Sra J. Espinosa Ulloa,
Mexico City
70. **Senora Carmen T. de Carillo
Gil** 1944
Oil on canvas / 85×60
Coll: Sra C.T. de L. Carrillo Gil,
Mexico City
71. **Archbishop Luis Martinez** 1944
Tempera on canvas / 102×74 / OF
72. **Self Portrait** 1946
Oil on canvas / 65×55 / CG
73. **Self Portrait** n.d.
Tempera on canvas / 56×46 /
INBA, Museo de Arte Moderno,
Mexico City
74. **Model** n.d.
Tempera / 49.5×33.5 / OF
75. **Study for Portrait of Sra
Martino** n.d.
Tempera / 55×40 / OF

**Scenes from
Popular Life
1941-c.1946**

76. **Beggars** 1941
Tempera on canvas / 39×54 / CG
77. **Four Women** 1942
Oil on canvas / 42×33 / CG
78. **Three Women** 1942
Tempera / 27.8×40 / CG
79. **Workers' Bar** 1942
Oil on masonite / 59.3×79.7 / CG
80. **Mexican Bar** 1942-3
Tempera / 28×37.5 / CG
81 **Head of a Coquette** 1943
Tempera / 50×35
Coll: Ing. & Sra J. Espinosa
Ulloa, Mexico City
82. **The Slum Girls** 1943
(Las Changuitas)
Watercolour / 39.2×57.2 / CG

83. **Quarrel in a Bar** 1944
Oil on masonite / 60.5×80.5 / CG
84. **Seated Woman** 1944
Tempera / 39×30 / CG
85. **The Mad Woman** 1944
Etching & drypoint / 27×17.5 / CG
86. **The Cabbages** 1944
Oil on canvas / 98.5×118.5 / CG
87. **Cripple** 1944
Aquatint / 18×13 / CG
88. **The Unemployed** 1944
Aquatint / 22.5×16.5 / CG
89. **Contortionists** 1944
Etching & aquatint / 30×44.5 / CG
90. **Clown** 1944
Aquatint & etching / 270×170 / CG
91. **Clown in Lines** 1944
Drypoint / 27×21.5 / CG
92. **The Clown and the World** 1944
Etching & aquatint / 27×22 / CG
93. **Woman** 1945
Ink / 28.5×43.5 / CG
94. **Three Women** 1945
Ink / 46×31 / CG
95. **Head of a Woman** 1945
Oil on paper / 59×37 / OF
96. **Peasants & Figures** 1945
Ink / 51×67 / OF
97. **Convivial** 1945
Ink / 50×70 / OF
98. **Woman in Green** 1946
Tempera / 56.7×44.1 / CG
99. **Woman with Quiff
against blue background** n.d.
Tempera / 50×32.5 / OF
100. **Model with Quiff** n.d.
Tempera / 35×26 / OF
101. **Two Models with Quiffs** n.d.
Tempera / 38×56 / OF
102. **Model in Greens
and Ochres** n.d.
Tempera / 37×29 / OF
103. **Woman Thinking** n.d.
Tempera / 68×50 / CG
104. **Three Prostitutes** n.d.
Tempera / 35.5×53 / OF
105. **Beggar Woman** n.d.
Tempera / 28×39 / OF
106. **Bar Room Scene** n.d.
Gouache / 45×63
Coll: Ing. P. Gutiérrez Roldán
107. **Popular Bar Room Scene** n.d.
Pencil / 20×29 / OF
108. **Nude and Three Heads** n.d.
Pencil / 20×39 / OF

Late Studies

109. **Torso** 1943
Tempera / 38×55 / OF
110. **Nude Lying Down** 1943
Tempera / 39×56 / OF
111. **Cadaver** 1943
Charcoal / 55×37.5 / CG
112. **Madness** 1945
Ink / 35×38 / CG
113. **The Devil** 1945
Ink / 44×29 / OF
114. **Four Reclining Figures** 1945
Ink / 44×29.5 / CG

115. **Group of Figures** 1945
Ink / 45×58 / OF
116. **Headless Woman** 1945
Ink / 51×34 / OF
117. **Head and two hands** 1945
Ink / 67×50 / OF
118. **Jagged Form** 1945
Ink / 50×33 / OF
119. **Female Nude** 1946
Tempera / 68×48 / CG
120. **Hoodwinked** 1948
Tempera, ink & crayon / 76×55 /
OF
121. **The Tricksters** 1948
Crayon / 66×98 / CG
122. **Head with Nose Uppermost**
1948
Charcoal, crayon, ink /
62.5×48 / OF
123. **Legs** 1949
Charcoal / 48×62 / OF
124. **Nude** n.d.
Tempera / 55×41.5 / OF
125. **Study for 'Las Indias'** n.d.
Charcoal / 44.5×32 / OF
126. **Nude Leaning on Hands** n.d.
Charcoal / 50×65 / OF
127. **Models with Apples** n.d.
Charcoal / 62×49 / OF
128. **Nude Leaning on Left Arm** n.d.
Charcoal / 50×65 / OF
129. **Female Nude** n.d.
Charcoal / 48×62 / OF
130. **Sketch of a Woman** n.d.
Charcoal / 50×33
Private collection, Mexico
131. **Hands** n.d.
Charcoal / 45.5×41 / CG
132. **Four Interlaced Figures** n.d.
Ink / 29×37 / OF

**Satirical,
Anti-Military and
Anti-Clerical
Subjects
1944-1947**

133. **Victory** 1944
Oil on masonite / 50×60 / CG
134. **Small Nation** 1944
Oil and tempera on canvas /
49.5×64.5 / OF
135. **Clowns** 1945
Ink / 29 3 44 / OF
136. **Clowns of War** 1945
Ink / 50×69 / OF
137. **Military Men** 1945
Ink / 50×60 / OF
138. **Don Juan** 1945
Gouache / 52×45.5 / CG
139. **Perfume and Pomade** 1946
Oil on canvas / 49.5×64.2 / CG
140. **Don Juan Tenorio** 1946
Oil on canvas / 60.3×73.5 / CG
141. **Demagogue** 1946
Oil and tempera on canvas /
78×61 / OF

142. **The Tyrant** 1947
Oil and tempera on canvas /
92×65
INBA, Museo de Arte Moderno,
Mexico City
143. **Military Satire** n.d.
Oil and tempera on canvas /
58×37 / OF

144. **Designs for Three Ballets**
145. **1945**
146. Tempera / 47×60; 49.7×66.8;
48.5×69.5 / CG
147. **Two Designs for the Ballet
'Umbral'** 1945
148. Backcloth: Four Figures and
Mask; Two Ballerinas.
Gouache / 38×48.5 / 37×48
Coll: Galéria Arvil, Mexico City
At this time Orozco made designs
for four different works for the
Ballet de la Ciudad de México.

**Two Illustrations for
John Steinbeck's novel,
'The Pearl', 1947**

149. **Submerged Man**
Ink / 37×29 / OF
150. **The Family**
Ink / 44.5×29 / OF

**Thirteen Drawings
from the series 'Truth'
1945**

151. **Devious Figure**
Ink / 50×67 / OF
152. **Nude and Arm**
Ink / 68×50 / OF
153. **Three Interlaced Figures and
Figure with Cap**
Ink / 34×33 / OF
154. **Contorted Nudes**
Ink / 29×44 / OF
155. **The Adult Icarus**
Ink / 29×44 / OF
156. **Satire on Militarism**
Ink / 44×29 / OF
157. **Two Mounted Figures**
Ink / 44.5×29.5 / OF
158. **Mounted, Winged Figure**
Ink / 44×29.6 / OF
159. **The Rich and the Poor**
Ink / 46.5×68 / OF
160. **Untitled**
Ink / 47×36 / OF
161. **Untitled**
Ink / 36×47 / OF
162. **Torso, Head and Legs**
Ink / 59×44 / OF
163. **Justice**
Ink / 34.5×51.5 / OF

**Two Drawings
from the series
'Demagogy'
1948**

164. **Head**
Charcoal and crayon /
62.5×48.3 / 48.3 / OF
165. **Profile of Head**
Charcoal and crayon /
62.5×48.3 / OF

**Five drawings
from the series
'Conservative
Oppression' 1948**

166. **Confession**
Charcoal and crayon /
62.5×46.5 / OF
167. **Procession**
Charcoal and crayon /
50.2×47.5 / OF
168. **Head with Key**
Charcoal and crayon /
48.2×63.6 / OF
169. **Copulation I**
Charcoal and crayon /
48.5×62.6 / OF
170. **Copulation II**
Charcoal and crayon /
48.5×62.6 / OF

Slaves
These works are all linked to the
subject matter of the mural
**Hidalgo: The Great Mexican
Revolutionary Legislation and
the Abolition of Slavery**
1948 - painted on the ceiling of
the Chamber of Deputies in the
Palace of Government,
Guadalajara, Mexico. All are
dated 1948.

171. **Slave** (cloths and ropes)
Charcoal / 63×48 / OF
172. **Study for Slave**
Charcoal / 63×48 / OF
173. **Head of Slave with Key**
Charcoal / 71×53 / OF
174. **Head Covered with Cloths,
Chains and a Cardinal's Hat**
Charcoal / 62.5×48.5 / OF
175. **Slave with Crown and Barbs**
Charcoal / 71×53.5 / OF
176. **Cardinals' Hats and Bishops'
Mitres**
Charcoal, crayon, ink / 67.5×53 /
OF
177. **Slave**
Crayon, and tempera / 76×56 /
OF
178. **Slave**
Piroxiline on masonite /
209×122 / OF
Piroxiline is a commercially
produced synthetic paint that
both Orozco and Siqueiros used
during the 1940s.

**Los Teules —
the White Gods
Skulls, Masks and
the Indian Past
1947 - 49**

179. **Los Teules No.1** 1947
The Leap of Alvarado
Tempera on masonite /
70×112 / CG
180. **Los Teules No.3** 1947
Cortez directing the battle
Tempera on masonite /
77.5×101 / CG
181. **Los Teules No.4** 1947
Piroxiline on masonite /
121.7×159 / CG
182. **Jagged Skull** 1947
Piroxiline on masonite /
150×122 / OF
183. **Hide in Blue** 1947
(Piel en Azul)
Piroxilene on masonite /
168×122 / OF
184. **Indians** 1947
Piroxiline on masonite /
193×122 / OF
185. **Wounded Indian** 1947
Piroxiline on masonite /
172×122 / OF
186. **Mask with Butterfly** 1947
Piroxiline on masonite /
95×132 / OF
187. **The Drowned** 1947
Piroxiline on masonite /
122×173 / OF
188. **The Dismembered Man** 1947
Piroxiline on masonite /
160×122 / OF
189. **Head Pierced by Arrows** 1947
Piroxiline on masonite /
122×173 / OF
190. **Obese Figure with
Skeleton and Skull** 1948
Charcoal / 69×52 / OF
191. **Obese Figure with Skull** 1948
Charcoal / 68×49 / OF
192. **Mask** 1948
Charcoal / 63×49 / OF
193. **Mask** 1949
Ink / 56×38 / OF

**Religious,
Symbolic and
Allegorical
Subjects**

194. **Christ Destroying his Cross**
1943
Oil on canvas / 93×130 / CG
195. **The Martyrdom of Saint
Sebastian** 1943
Tempera / 38.5×55.5 / CG
A larger version is in the Vatican
Museum
196. **Death and Resurrection** 1943
Tempera on masonite /
122×177 / OF

197. **Prometheus** 1944
Oil on canvas / 79×93 / CG
198. **Icarus** c.1945
Tempera / 58×37 / OF
199. **Man with Cap, Nero** 1946
Tempera / 45.5×29 / OF
200. **Landscape of Peaks** 1948
Oil and tempera on masonite /
100×125.5× CG
201. **Vigil** 1948
Piroxiline on masonite /
207×122 / OF
202. **Hand** 1948
Piroxiline on masonite /
214×122 / OF
203. **Metaphysical Landscape** 1948
Piroxiline on masonite /
215×122 / OF

Studies for Murals

**The National
Preparatory School
Murals
1923-1926**

204. **Study of Six Figures and a
Running Man; detail from
Spring** 1923
Pencil / 39.5×45 / INBA
205. **Running Man;
Detail from 'Spring'** 1923
Pencil / 38×30 / INBA
206. **Male Torso** 1923
Pencil / 57.8×46.5 / INBA
207. **Foot with Sunflower** 1923
Pencil / 60×50 / INBA

The next two items
are sketches for
'Maternity' 1923

208. **Head of Boy with Arm** 1923
Pencil / 62×50 / INBA
209. **Hand**
Pencil / 50×58 / INBA
210. **Justice** 1923-4
Pencil / 38×46 / OF
211. **Catholic Womanhood;
detail from The Reactionary
Forces** 1923-24
Pencil / 35.3×80 / INBA
212. **The Eternal Father;
detail from The Last
Judgment**
Pencil / 30.5×50 / INBA
213. **Franciscan Friar** 1923-24
Ink / 38×28 / OF
214. **Three Women** 1923
Pencil / 32.5×42.5 / INBA
215. **Feet** 1923
Crayon / 33×42 / OF
216. **Woman in Profile with Raised
Arm** 1923
Charcoal / 55×49 / OF
217. **Joined Hands** 1923
Pencil / 41×50 / OF

218. **Study of Two Arms** 1924
Pencil / 65×50 / INBA
219. **Three Indians** 1923-26
Pencil / 37×52 / OF
220. **Interlaced Hands** 1923-26
Pencil / 33×50 / OF
221. **Hand in Response** 1923-26
Charcoal / 38.5×34 / OF
222. **Hand** 1923-26
223. **Soldier's Greeting** 1926
Pencil / 49×57 / OF
224. **Soldier** 1926
Pencil / 32.5×25 / OF
225. **Peasant Woman with Plough**
1926
Pencil / 33×50 / OF
226. **Head of a Woman with Closed
Eyes** 1926
Pencil / 39.5×45 / INBA
227. **Head of a Smiling Woman**
1923-26
Pencil / 47×60 / INBA
228. **Head of Man Drinking Water**
1923-26
Pencil / 64×64 / OF
229. **The Strike** 1926
Pencil / 55×41 / OF
230. **The Trench** 1926
Pencil / 55×48 / OF

**'Omniciencia'
1925 Mural in
the Casa de los
Azulejos
('House of Tiles')
Mexico City
1925**

231. **Study with Seven Figures
(first sketch)** 1925
Pencil / 70×50 / INBA
232. **Study on the Creation of Man**
Pencil / 23.5×45 / INBA
233. **Head of a Woman with Braids**
Pencil / 99×70 / INBA
234. **Study of Head and Hands**
Pencil / 99.5×70 / INBA

**Social Revolution
Mural at
Industrial School,
Orizaba, Veracruz,
Mexico, 1926**

235. **Soldiers and Workers**
Pencil / 33×50 / OF
236. **Workers and their Families**
Pencil / 33×50 / OF

**Prometheus
Mural in Frary Hall,
Pomona College,
Claremont, California,
1930**

237. **Prometheus**
Pencil / 45×57.5 / OF

238. **Prometheus** 1935
Drypoint / 16.5× 22.5 / CG
As he had with the Preparatory
School subjects, Orozco made a
print based on the main motif of
the Pomona mural some four
years after its completion.

**New School
for Social Research,
New York,
1930**

239. **Lenin**
Pencil / 36×49 / OF
240. **Gandhi**
Pencil / 36×44 / OF
241. **Slaves**
Pencil / 36×45 / OF

**The Native World
and the American World
Before and Since
the Advent of
Industrialisation.
Murals in
the Baker Library,
Dartmouth College,
Hanover,
New Hampshire,
USA,
1932-34**

242. **Migration; first panel**
Pencil./ 59.5×47.5 / OF
243. **Indian Head; (detail)**
Pencil / 59.5×47.5 / OF
244. **Ancient Human Sacrifice;**
second panel
Tempera / 52×35 / CG
245. **Detail of Second Panel**
Charcoal / 52×37 / OF
246. **Heads of Aztec Warriors;**
detail of third panel
Tempera / 37×48 / OF
247. **The Coming of Quetzalcoatl**
Fourth panel
Pencil / 43.5×53 / OF
248. **Detail of fourth panel**
Pencil / 45×57 / OF
249. **Serpents' Heads;**
Detail of sixth panel: The
Departure of Quetzalcoatl
Pencil / 36.5×48 / OF
250. **Forebodings 1935**
Drypoint / 15×18 / CG
Based on cat.249
251. **Torso with bent shoulder;**
detail of sixth panel
Pencil / 48×61 / OF
252. **Head of Hernan Cortez; detail**
of eighth panel:
Cortez and the Cross
Pencil / 52×36 / OF
253. **Conquest and Evangelism;**
detail from eighth panel
Tempera / 40×45 / OF
254. **Hispano-America; eleventh**
panel
Pencil / 50×35.5 / OF
255. **Christ Destroying His Cross;**
detail of fourteenth panel:
Modern Migration of the
Spirit
Pencil / 47.5×52 / OF
256. **Left Foot of Christ;**
Detail of fourteenth panel
Pencil / 47.5×53.5 / OF
257. **Head of Rebel**
Pencil / 35×65 / OF
258. **The Industrial World**
Pencil / 51×38.5 / OF

Works based on
'Catharsis'
Mural
painted in 1934,
in the Palace
of Fine Arts,
Mexico City

259. **La Chata (Snubnose)** 1935
Drypoint / 19.5×14.5 / CG
260. **Woman No.1** 1935
Litho / 31×43 / CG
261. **Two Heads and Machines**
1935
Litho / 31×43.5 / CG

'Creative Man'
and 'The People and
its False Leaders'
Two murals
painted in
the Assembly Hall
of the University of
Guadalajara, 1936

262. **Detail from**
the Victims; side panel
Tempera / 70×33 / OF
263. **Cadaver and Two Hands**
Detail from back panel
Pencil / 28×45 / OF
264. **Sketch for Complete Cupola**
Pencil / 57×43 / OF
265. **The Philosopher-Teacher**
Pencil / 38×56 / OF
266. **The Worker**
Pencil / 28.5×31 / OF

'Hidalgo and
National Independence'
Mural on
the principal staircase
of the Palace
of Government,
Guadalajara, 1937

267. **Hidalgo**
Tempera / 59×56.5 / OF
268. **Hands of Hidalgo**
Tempera / 13.5×50 / OF
269. **Hands of Hidalgo**
Pencil / 56×46 / OF

Humanity, Mexico Before
and After the Spanish
Conquest. Man and His Urge
to Better Himself. Murals in
the Deconsecrated Chapel of
the Hospicio Cabanas,
Guadalajara, 1938-39

270. **The Mechanised Masses**
Tempera / 63×48 / OF
271. **Suffering Humanity**
Tempera / 55×37 / OF
272. **The Scientific**
Tempera / 63×48 / OF
273. **The City in Flames**
Tempera / 55×37 / OF
274. **The Conquered**
Pencil / 54×40 / OF
275. **The Baroque**
Tempera / 54×36 / OF
276. **Hernan Cortez**
Tempera / 74×25 / OF
277. **Hernan Cortez**
(related easel study)
Oil on canvas / 91×70 / Coll: Lic.
G. Martínez Domínguez, Mexico
City
278. **The American Religions**
Tempera / 33.5×57.5 / OF
279. **Horses of the Conquest**
Tempera / 33×66 / OF
280. **Philip II**
Tempera / 56×25 / OF

Studies for
the Cupola:

281. **Head**
Charcoal / 63×47 / OF
282. **Reclining Figure**
Pencil / 48×62 / OF
283. **Man of Fire**
Pencil / 55×39 / OF

Miscellaneous Studies:

284. **Horses**
Tempera / 38×57 / OF
285. **Three Legs**
Charcoal / 70×50 / OF
286. **Kneeling Figure**
Charcoal / 62×48 / OF
287. **Figures**
Tempera / 45×34 / OF
288. **Evangelism**
Tempera / 34×57 / OF

'Justice and False Justice.
National Wealth
Proletarian Struggle'
Murals in
the Supreme Court of
Justice,
Mexico City,
1941

289. **Justice**
Pencil / 33×68 / OF
290. **Detail from 'Justice'**
Tempera / 49×34 / OF
291. **Man's Head against the Floor**
Tempera / 41×58 / OF
292. **National Wealth**
Pencil / 33×68 / OF

'Allegory of
the Modern Apocalypse
in relation to Our Times'
Murals on the west wall
and two western vaults
of the nave of
the Iglesia del Hospital de
Jesús,
Mexico City, 1942 - 44

293. **The Devil** 1943
Tempera / 33.5×50 / OF
294. **The Hydra with Seven Heads**
1944
Tempera / 36×49 / OF
295. **Study for Mural** 1944
Tempera / 55×47 / OF

**'The Defeat of Ignorance'
and 'The People Draw near
to the Doors of the School'**

**Two murals in the hall of
the Escuela Nacional de
Maestros,
Mexico City,
1947 -48**

296. **Study of Charcoal Burner's
Daughter** 1948
Charcoal and crayon / 64×49 / OF

**'Juárez, the Church and the
Imperialists.' Mural in the
Sala de Reforma,
Chapultepec Castle,
1948**

297. **Three Hands with Talons**
Charcoal / 62×48 / OF

**Projects
for Mural**
(not completed)
1949

298. **Curved Structures**
Ink, Charcoal and crayon /
102×58 / OF
299. **Geometrical Structures**
Ink, charcoal and crayon /
102×68 / OF

300. **Portrait of José Clemente
Orozco** 1947
by David Alfaro Siqueiros
Piroxiline on masonite /
121×100 / CG

Bibliography

Compiled by
James A. Findlay

Writings by Orozco
Books

Orozco, José Clemente. **Apuntes autobiográficos.** México DF: Secretaría de Educación Pública, Subsecretaría de Asuntos Culturales 1966. 127pp.

Orozco, José Clemente. **The artist in New York: letters to Jean Charlot and unpublished writings, 1925 - 1929.** Austin, Texas: University of Texas Press 1974. 99pp. Translated by Ruth L. C. Simms

Orozco, José Clemente. **El artista en Neuva York; (cartas a Jean Charlot, 1925 - 1929, y tres textos inéditos).** México DF: Siglo XXI; 1971. 187pp.

Orozco, José Clemente. **Autobiografía.** México DF: Ediciones Occidente, 1945. 156pp.

Orozco, José Clemente. **Autobiografía.** Nueva ed. México DF: Ediciones Era, 1970. 126pp.

Orozco, José Clemente. **An autobiography.** Austin, Texas: University of Texas Press, 1962. 171pp. Translated by Robert C. Stephenson

Orozco, José Clemente. **Orozco 'explains'.** New York: Museum of Modern Art, 1940. 12pp. Also published in The Bulletin of The Museum of Modern Art. 7(4): 1 - 12; August 1940

Orozco, José Clemente. **Textos de Orozco: con un estudio y un apendice por Justino Fernándéz.** México DF: Imprenta Universitaria, 1955. 157pp. Partial text in Spanish and English

Parts of Books

Orozco, José Clemente. *Artículo de José Clemente Orozco.* In: Lozano, Rodríguez. Rodríguez Lozano. México DF: Clardecor, 1949: 9 - 10

Orozco, José Clemente. *Cartas de Orozco.* In: Carrillo Gil, Alvar. Obras de José Clemente Orozco en la Colección Carrillo Gil, México: complemento y notas del Dr Alvar Carrillo Gil. México DF, 1953: 233 - 253

Orozco, José Clemente. *Cartas de Orozco a J.G.Ugarte, J.J.Crespo de la Serna, L.E.Schmeckebier, y L.Cardoza y Aragón.* In: Cardoza y Aragón, Luis. Orozco. México DF: Instituto de Investigaciones Estéticas, Universidad Nacional Autónoma de México, 1959: 275 - 314

Orozco, José Clemente. *Fragmento de una carta a Justino Fernández, Jiquilpan, Mick., Agosto 31, 1940.* In: Fernández, Justino. Orozco: forma e idea. México DF: Libreria de Porrúa, 1942: 15

Orozco, José Clemente. *Fragmentos de una carta a Rafael García Granados, Presidente de la 'Sociedad de Estudios Cortesianos', Mexico DF, octubre 23, 1941.* In: Fernández, Justino. Orozco: forma e idea. México DF: Libreria de Porrúa, 1942: 32 - 33

Orozco, José Clemente. *General Report of the Mexican Delegation to the American Artists' Congress.* First American Artists' Congress; 14 - 16 February 1936, New York City. New York: American Artists' Congress, 97 - 99

Orozco, José Clemente. *Notas: (de carácter informativo y técnico).* In: El Colegio Nacional, México DF José Clemente Orozco: sexta exposición. 1948

Orozco, José Clemente. *Notas acerca de la técnica de la pintura mural en México en los últimos 25 anos.* In: Instituto Nacional de Bellas Artes y Literature, Secretaría de Educación Pública, México DF. José Clemente Orozco: exposición nacional. México DF 1947

Orozco, José Clemente. *Preface.* In: Dickerson, Albert I., ed. Orozco frescoes at Dartmouth. Hanover, NH: Dartmouth College, 1934

Orozco, José Clemente. *Preface.* In: Hale, Gardner. Fresco painting. New York: William Edwin Rudge, 1933

Periodicals

Orozco, José Clemente. *Autobiografía de José Clemente Orozco.* Excelsior (México DF). Febrero 17, 20, 24, 27; Marzo 3, 6, 10, 13, 17, 21, 24, 27, 31; Abril 3, 8, 1942. A series of newspaper articles

Orozco, José Clemente. *Una carta del dibujante Orozco.* El Nacional. 1916 septiembre 20; 3

Orozco, José Clemente. *A correction.* Mexican Folkways. 5(1):8 - 9; January - March 1929. Text in English and Spanish

Orozco, José Clemente. *An eruption of paint.* Harper's. 225(1347):45 - 50; August 1962

Orozco, José Clemente. *Fragments of an autobiography.* Magazine of Art. 45:347 - 354; December 1952

Orozco, José Clemente. *The heritage of the Mexican child.* Everyday Art. 12(3):9 - 10; February - March 1934

Orozco, José Clemente. *Mensaje a la UNESCO por radio.* Tiras de Colores (México DF). 6(59); enero 1948

Orozco, José Clemente. *New world, new races, new art.* Creative Art. 4(1):44 - 46; January 1929

Orozco, José Clemente. *No es una improvisación el ballet organizado aquí: lo estuvieron preparando 10 anos y es una 'realidad indestructible'.* Excelsior (México DF) 21 marzo 1945

Orozco, José Clemente. *Rojo: publicación mensual de artes plásticas.* Guadalajara, Jalisco, México: Unión de Pintores y Escultores de Jalisco. 1; 1 marzo 1934. Collaborator

Orozco, José Clemente. *A vast fresco.* Art Digest. 6(17):5; 1 June 1932. Statement by Orozco regarding Dartmough mural 'Man released from the Mechanistic'

Books Illustrated by Orozco

Azuela, Mariano. *The Under Dogs (Los de Abajo).* New York: Bretano's, 1929 224pp.

Campobello, Nellie. *Mis libros.* México DF: Cía General de Ediciones; 1960. 514pp.

Smith, Susan. *The glories of Venus: a novel of modern Mexico.* New York: Harper, 1931. 263pp.

Steinbeck, John. *The Pearl.* New York: The Viking Press, 1947

Velásquez Andrade, Manuel. *Cuadros vivos.* Tlaxcala, México: Ediciones Gamma, 1936

Periodicals Illustrated by Orozco

L'abc. México DF, 1925

El Hijo del Ahuizote. México DF, 1912
El Machete. México DF, 1924

La Vanguardia. Orizaba, Veracruz, México, 1915

Books on Orozco

Cardoza y Aragón, Luis. *José Clemente Orozco.* Buenos Aires: Losado, 1944. 58pp. (Monografias de Arte Americano. Serie Americana 1)

Cardoza y Aragón, Luis. *José Clemente Orozco: pinturas murales en la Universidad de Guadalajara, Jalisco.* México DF: Imprenta Mundial, 1937. 47pp.

Cardoza y Aragón, Luis. *Orozco.* México DF: Instituto de Investigaciones Estéticas, Universidad Nacional Autónoma de México, 1959. 315pp.

Cardoza y Aragón, Luis. *Orozco.* 2ª ed. México DF: Universidad Nacional Autónoma de México, Dirección General de Publicaciones, 1974. 182pp.

Castro Leal, Antonio. *José Clemente Orozco (con una conferencia de Antonio Castro Leal).* México DF, 1947. 4pp. (Cuaderno de artes plásticas. Tiras de colores)

Colegio Nacional, México DF. *Homenaje de El Colegio Nacional al pintor José Clemente Orozco, 14 de diciembre de 1949*. México DF: Ediciones de El Colegio Nacional, 1949? 25pp. Speeches by Silvio A. Zavala and Manuel Toussaint

Cuesta, Jorge. *José Clemente Orozco*. México DF; 1939. (Galería de pintores modernos mexicanos, no.3)

del Guerico, Antonio. *José Clemente Orozco*. Milano: Fabbri. 1966. 23pp. (I Maestri del Colore, 200).

Dickerson, Albert I., ed. *The Orozco frescoes at Dartmouth*. Hanover, NH: Dartmouth College, 1934. 24pp.

Dickerson, Albert I., ed. *The Orozco frescoes at Dartmouth*. Hanover, NH: Dartmouth College, 1962. 24pp. Re-issue of 1934 edition, with colour cover

Echavarría, Salvador. *Orozco: Hospicio Cabañas*. Guadalajara, México: Planeación y Promoción; 1959. 61pp. Text in Spanish and English

8 lithographs: murals at Jiquilpan. Jiquilpan, Mexico? 1941? 8pp.

Fernández, Justino. *Los grabados de Orozco: 17 láminas tiradas por Carlas Alvarado Lang*. México DF, 1951

Fernández, Justino. *José Clemente Orozco: 10 reproducciones en color de pinturas murales*. México DF: Fischgrund, 1944. Text in Spanish and English

Fernández, Justino. *José Clemente Orozco: forma e idea*. México DF: Libreria de Porrúa, 1942. 209pp.

Fernández, Justino. *José Clemente Orozco: forma e idea*. 2ª ed. México DF: Porrúa; 1956. 221pp. Revised and enlarged edition with additional illustrations of post-1942 works and extended bibliography

Fernández, Justino. *José Clemente Orozco: 10 reproductions of his mural paintings*. Mexico City: Eugenio Fischgrund, Modern Art Editions, 1944. 14pp.

Fernández, Justino. *José Clemente Orozco: the painter of our time*. Mexico City: E. Fischgrund, Modern Art Editions, 1944

Fernández, Justino. *Orozco: Universidad de Guadalajara*. Guadalajara, Jal., México: Planeación y Promoción, 1960. 43pp. Text in Spanish and English

Flaccus, Kimball, ed. *Orozco at Dartmouth: a symposium*. Hanover, NH: Arts Press, 1933. (The Arts Chapbooks, no.4)

Gamboa, Fernando. *José Clemente Orozco*. México DF: Ediciones de Arte, 1948. 68pp. (Colección Anahuac de Arte Mexicano, v.3). Text in Spanish, English, French, and Italian

Helm, MacKinley. *Man of fire: J.C.Orozco, an interpretative memoir*. Boston: The Institute of Contemporary Art; New York: Harcourt, Brace, 1953. 245pp.

Helm, MacKinley. *Man of fire: J.C.Orozco, an interpretative memoir*. Westport, Connecticut: Greenwood Press, 1971. Reprint of 1953 edition

Hopkins, Jon H. *Orozco: a catalogue of his graphic work*. Flagstaff, Arizona: Northern Arizona University Publications, 1967. 136pp.

Hurlburt, Laurance P. *José Clemente Orozco at the New School for Social Research and Dartmouth College: 1930-1934*. Madison, Wisconsin: University of Wisconsin, 1971. 147pp. Master's thesis

Instituto Nacional de Bellas Artes, México DF. *Museo José Clemente Orozco*. México DF, 1958. 33pp.

Instituto Nacional de Bellas Artes, México DF *Museo-Taller José Clemente Orozco en Guadalajara, Jalisco: la casa del artista convertida en museo en homenaje a la obra del gran pintor desaparecido*. México DF, 197?. 22pp.

José Clemente Orozco: homenaje en ocasión del 1er aniversario de la fundación del Museo Taller, dedicado a su memoria, Guadalajara, Jal. México DF: Munoz Galache; 1952. 22pp.

Kostenevich, Al'bert Grigor'evich. *Kh.K.Orosko*. Leningrad: Izdatel'stvo Iskusstvo, Leningradskoe Otdelenie; 1969. 189pp. Text in Russian

Lynch, James. *José Clemente Orozco: the easel paintings and the graphic art*. Cambridge, Massachusetts: Harvard University, 1960. Dissertation

Marrozzini, Luigi, ed. *Catálogo completo de la obra gráfica de Orozco*. San Juan, Puerto Rico: Instituto de Cultura Puertorriquena, Universidad de Puerto Rico, 1970? 132pp. Partial text in Spanish and English

Mérida, Carlos. *Frescoes in Palacio de Justicia [Mexico City] and Jiquilpan [Michoacán] by C. Orozco: an interpretative guide with 19 reproductions*. México DF: Frances Toor Studios, 1943. 16pp. (Mexican art series, 11)

Mérida, Carlos. *Orozco's frescoes in Guadalajara*. México DF: Frances Toor Studios, 1940. 12pp. Photographs by Juan Arauz Lomeli. Edited by Frances Toor.

Museo Nacional de Artes Plásticas, México DF. *Museo-Taller José Clemente Orozco en Guadalajara, Jal. . . . la casa del artista convertida en museo en homenaje a la obra del gran pintor desaparecido*. México DF, 1951? 16pp

Obras de José Clemente Orozco en la Colección Carrillo Gil, México: catálogo y notas de Justino Fernández. México DF, 1949. 222pp.

Obras de José Clemente Orozco en la Colección Carrillo Gil, México: complemento y notas del Dr. Alvar Carrillo Gil. México DF, 1953. 297pp.

Orozco en color. México; 1949? 26pp.

Ramos García, Luis. *José Clemente Orozco en Guadalajara*. Guadalajara, Jalisco, México

Reed, Alma, ed. *José Clemente Orozco*. New York: William Edwin Rudge, 1932.

Reed, Alma. *Orozco*. México DF: Fondo de Cultura Económica, 1955. 349pp. Spanish translation of Oxford University Press, 1956 edition

Reed, Alma. *Orozco*. New York: Oxford University Press, 1956. 308pp.

Reed, Alma. *Orozco*. México DF: Fondo de Cultura Económica, 1958. 352pp. Spanish translation of Oxford University Press, 1956 edition

Reed, Alma. *Orozco: José Clemente Orozco*. Dresden: VEB Verlag der Kunst; 1979. 386pp. German translation of 1956 Oxford University Press edition

Sánchez Gutiérrez, Edmundo. *José Clemente Orozco*. México DF: Fischgrund, 1941. 24pp.

Secretaría de Educación Pública, México. *Frescoes de José Clemente Orozco en la Universidad de Dartmouth (EUA)*. México: Secretaría de Educación Pública, 1944. 24pp.

Secretaría de Educación Pública, México. *imágenes de la revolución*. México: Secretaría de Educación Pública, Departamento de Bellas Artes, 1934? 8pp.

Zuno, José Guadalupe. *José Clemente Orozco: el pintor ironista*. Guadalajara, México: Universidad de Guadalajara, 1962. 221pp.

Zuno, José Guadalupe. *Orozco y la ironía plástica*. México DF: Ediciones Cuadernos Americanos, 1953. 85pp.

Orozco Exhibition Catalogues

Casa Francisco Navarro, México DF *Exposición José Clemente Orozco, del 1 al 20 de septiembre de 1916, en la Ave. Francisco I. Madero, Núm. 28, Casa Francisco Navarro: estudios de mujeres*

Bernheim-Jeune, Paris. José Clemente Orozco: exposition d'oeuvres récentes, du lundi 14 décembre au jeudi 24 décembre 1925 . . . Invitation

Galleries of Marie Sterner, New York. *Ink and pencil drawings from a series 'Mexico in revolution' by José Clemente Orozco, October 10 to 22, 1928*

Art Students' League, New York. *Paintings & drawings by José Clemente Orozco, April 15th - 30th, 1929*

Delphic Studios, New York. *Exhibition of recent paintings by José Clemente Orozco, February 3rd to February 25th, 1930*

Los Angeles Museum. Exposition Park, Los Angeles. *Lithographs by José Clemente Orozco, October, 1930*

Downtown Gallery, New York. *Exhibition of works of José Clemente Orozco, March-April 1931*

Delphic Studios, New York. *José Clemente Orozco*. 1932. Introduction by Alma Reed

Civic Auditorium, La Porte, Indiana. *Exhibition of lithographs, mural studies, photographs of frescoes, paintings, drawings by José Clemente Orozco, April 6th to 29th, 1934.* Assembled and arranged by Mrs Alma Reed, Director, Delphic Studios, New York City

Arts Club of Chicago. *José Clemente Orozco: [exhibition] catalogue, paintings, drawings, lithographs, May - June, 1934.* Works selected by Alma Reed, Director of the Delphic Studios, New York.

Galería de Arte Mexicano, México DF. *Exposición de grabados originales . . . del 6 al 16 de junio de 1935.*

ACA Gallery, New York. *Two papers presented at the American Artists' Congress, February 15, 1936, for the Mexican delegates by Orozco and Siqueiros, and the catalogue of the exhibition at the A.C.A. Gallery, 52W. 8th Street, New York City, February 24-March 7.* 14pp.

Galería de Arte Mexicano, México DF. *José Clemente Orozco: exposición de bocetos para pinturas murales y de otros estudios, 1 al 20 de marzo de 1940*

Museum of Modern Art, New York. *Noted Mexican artist paints fresco 'Dive Bomber' on walls of The Museum of Modern Art.* 1940? 2pp. Press release

Colegio Nacional, México DF. *Catálogo de la primera exposición de Orozco en El Colegio Nacional, 1943.* 1943. Text by Justino Fernández

Colegio Nacional, México DF. *20 dibujos de José Clemente Orozco de la exposición de agosto de 1945 en el Colegio Nacional, México, 1945.* Talleres Gráficos de la Nación; 1945. 21pp.

Secretaría de Educación Pública, México. *José Clemente Orozco: exposición nacional: notas acerca de la técnica de la pintura mural en los últimos 25 anos, por Orozco. México; 1947.* 15pp

Instituto Nacional de Bellas Artes, México DF. Exposición nacional de José Clemente Orozco: catálogo que el Instituto Nacional de Bellas Artes publica con motivo de la exposición nacional retrospectiva José Clemente Orozco. México: Secretaría de Educación Pública; 1947. 147pp.

Colegio Nacional, México DF. *Sexta exposición de obras recientes: estudios y bocetos para murales, 1947 - 1948.* 24pp.

Pan American Union, New York. *The graphic work of Orozco [exhibition, May 15 to June 20, 1952].* Washington DC; 8pp.

Institute of Contemporary Arts, Boston. *J.C.Orozco memorial exhibition.* 1952.

Marion Koogler McNay Art Institute, San Antonio, Texas, *José Clemente Orozco.* 1959. Text by John Palmer Leeper

Instituto Nacional de Bellas Artes, México DF. *José Clemente Orozco: exposición especial en la VI Bienal de Sao Paulo: catálogo.* 1961. 16pp.

Museum of Modern Art, New York. *Orozco: studies for the Dartmouth murals, November 1961 - January 1962.* 5pp. Exhibition checklist

Museum of Modern Art, New York. *(Fifty-eight studies for José Clemente Orozco's murals at Dartmouth College . . . November 22, 1961 - January 21, 1962.)* 2pp. Press release

Museo Nacional de Bellas Artes, Lima, Perú. *Orozco: muralista mexicano, homenaje en Lima, Perú, 1964.* Lima, Perú; 1964. 18pp.

Museum of Modern Art. International Council, New York. *José Clemente Orozco: forarbeider til freskene i Dartmouth College, 18 November - Desember 1964.* Oslo: kunstnerhes Hus, 1964. 16pp. (Katalog no. 271)

Borgenicht Gallery, New York. *Drawings by José Clemente Orozco, January 4 - 31, 1969.* 16pp.

Instituto Nacional de Bellas Artes, México DF. *José Clemente Orozco: obra gráfica: colección del Museo José Clemente Orozco, oct. - dic., 1977.* 12pp.

[Museo Nacional?] Havana, Cuba. *José Clemente Orozco (y el arte de la revolución mexicana.)* 1978. 12pp. Organised by the Instituto Nacional de Bellas Artes, México

Musée d'Art Moderne de la ville de Paris. *José Clemente Orozco, 1883 - 1949: (exposition, jusqu'au mai 13, 1979)*

Queens Museum, Flushing, New York. *José Clemente Orozco and Diego Rivera: paintings, drawings, and prints, September 15 - November 11, 1979.* 6pp.

Palacio de Bellas Artes, México DF. *Exposición nacional de homenaje a José Clemente Orozco con motivo del XXX aniversario de su fallecimiento, septiembre - diciembre, 1979.* 169pp.

Selected Periodical Articles on Orozco

Atl, Dr. Fecundidad. *América (México DF).* enero 1926

Baldinger, Wallace. Orozco's last murals. *Magazine of Art.* 43:42 - 7; February 1950

Benson, E. M. Orozco at Dartmouth College. *Nation.* 137(3566):546 - 47; 8 November 1933

Benson, E. M. Orozco in New England: Dartmouth College murals. *Magazine of Art.* 26(10):443 - 49; October 1933

Bold tradition. *Artweek.* 1:1,5; 8 May 1976

Brenner, Antia. A Mexican rebel. *The Arts.* 12:201 - 209; October. 1927

Brenner, Antia. Orozco, murals with meaning. *Creative Art.* 12(2):134 - 136; February 1933

Brenson, M. Orozco: Mexican conscience. *Art in America.* 67:77 - 9; September 1979

Cardoza y Aragón, Luis. Contradicciones de Orozco. *Cuadernos Americanos.* 17:217 - 224; 1958

Cardoza y Aragón, Luis. José Clemente Orozco: iniciación de su vida artística. *Cultura Universitaria (Venezuela).* 64:79 - 85; 1958

Cardoza y Aragón, Luis. José Clemente Orozco, pintor mexicano. *Revista Nacional de Cultura (Venezuela).* 2(22):125 - 40; 1940 septiembre: 2(23):121 - 32; octubre 1940

Cardoza y Aragón, Luis. La obra de Orozco en la Iglesia del Hospital de Jesús. *Cuadernos Americanos.* 15(3):247-251; mayo-junio 1944

Cardoza y Aragón, Luis. Orozco 70. *Cuadernos Americanos.* 29(4):233 - 238; 1970

Carpentier, Alejo. El arte de José Clemente Orozco. *Social (La Habana).* 10; octubre 1926

Castro Leal, Antonio. José Clemente Orozco en la exposición nacional de sus obras. *México en el Arte.* (6):39 - 59; diciembre 1948

Charlot, Jean. José Clemente Orozco. *Magazine of Art.* 40:259 - 63; November 1947

Charlot, Jean. José Clemente Orozco. *Mexican Life (Mexico).* 4(6):25 - 30; May 1928

Charlot, Jean. José Clemente Orozco, su obra monumental. *Forma (Mexico).* 2(6): 32 - 51; junio. 1928

Charlot, Jean. Orozco in New York. *College Art Journal.* 19(1):40-53; Fall 1959

Charlot, Jean. Orozco's stylistic evolution. *College Art Journal.* 9(2):148 - 57; Winter 1949 - 50

Collectors choice: Orozco. *Time.* 66(23): 88 - 89; 5 December 1955

Cosgrove, Stanley and Ayre, Robert. Conversation about Orozco. *Canadian Art.* 7(2):60 - 65; 1949 - 1950

Dauriac, J. P. José Clemente Orozco, Musée d'Art de la Ville de Paris: exposition. *Pantheon.* 37:223 - 4; July 1979

Deschamps, Madeleine. José Clemente Orozco: une beauté du combat. *Art Press International.* (28):16 - 17; Mai 1979

Drawings and lithographs by Orozco. *Milwaukee Art Institute.* Bulletin. 3:6 - 7; April 1930

Echavarría, S. José Clemente Orozco en Guadalajara. *Artes de México.* (94 - 95): 104 - 21; 1967

Egleson, James. José Clemente Orozco. *Parnassus.* 12(7):5 - 10; November 1940

Eisenstein, Sergei. El Prometeo de la pintura mexicana. *América Latina (USSR).* pt.2: 159 - 66; 1978

Fernández, Justino. De una charla con José Clemente Orozco. *Anales del Instituto de Investigaciones Estéticas (México), Universidad Nacional de México.* 2(5):11 - 16; 1940

Fernández, Justino. Obras recientes de Orozco. *Hoy.* 349:59 - 61; 1943. 30 octubre 1930

Fernández, Justino. Obras recientes de Orozco. *Méxicano en el Arte.* (6):60 - 78; diciembre 1948

Fernández, Justino. Orozco: el pintor de nuestro tiempo. *Anales del Instituto de Investigaciones Estétcas (México), Universidad Nacional Autónoma de México.* 16:27-41; 1948

Fernández, Justino. Orozco, genius of America. *College Art Journal.* 9(2):142 - 47; Winter 1949 - 50

Fernández, Justino. Orozco's Zapata. *Chicago Art Institute Quarterly.* 45:62-5; November 1951

Fernández, Justino. Pinturas murales en el Museo de Historia. *Artes de México.* (92-93): 35; 1967

Fernández, Justino. Significación de Orozco. *Cuadernos Americanos.* 5(6); noviembre-diciembre 1946

Fernández, Justino. La trascendencia en la obra de Orozco. *Anales del Instituto de Investigaciones Estéticas. Universidad Nacional Autónoma de México.* 18:19-26; 1950.

Goodrich, Lloyd. The murals of the New School. *The Arts.* 17(6):399-403, 442-44, March 1931

Gray, Cleve. Orozco's recent frescoes. *Art in America.* 36:135-40; July 1948

Holmes, Jack D. L. A selected bibliography on José Clemente Orozco. *Inter-American Review of Bibliography.* (9):26-36; January 1960

José Clemente Orozco's Justice frescoes in Mexico City. *Magazine of Art.* 34:408-11; 1941

Kazaroveč, I. Khose Klemente Orosko [José Clemente Orozcol]. *Tvorcestvo.* (7):16-19; 1967

Kistler, A. New Lithographs. *Prints.* 6:96-7; December 1935

Lazo, Agustín. Nuevos frescoes de Clemente Orozco. *Forma (México).* 50(1):20-23; octubre 1926

López Oliva, Manuel. Cita con Orozco en La Habana. *Casa de las Américas.* 19(112): 128-132; enero-febrero 1979

Los Angeles: affaire Orozco. *Art News.* 52:48; September 1953

Moreno Galván, José María. Entre Orozco y Torres Garcia. *Goya.* 2:93-98; 1955-56

Mumford, Lewis. Orozco in New England. *New Republic.* 80(1036):231-35; 10 October 1934

Myers, Bernard. José Clemente Orozco: segunda parte, 1934-1940. *Artes de México.* 5(30):1-71; febrero 1960. Text in Spanish and English

Myers, Bernard. Murales de Orozco, 1923-32. *Artes de México.* 5(25):1-84; 1959. Text in Spanish and English

Neumeyer, Alfred. Orozco's mission. *College Art Journal.* 10(2):121-30; 1951

Orozco explains mural, Dive Bomber and Tank. *Art Digest.* 14:21; 1940 September. 1940

Orozco show banned in L.A. *Art Digest.* 27:14; August 1953

Orozco's Dive Bomber crashes into Tank at the Museum of Modern Art. *Art Digest.* 14:7; August 1940

Orozco's new job at Modern Museum. *Art Digest.* 14:26; July 1940

Patterson, R. H. The earliest Orozco print. *Library Chronical of the University of Texas at Austin.* 32-34: September 1972

Pearson, R. M. Orozco's latest mural. *Art Digest.* 23:30; 15 February 1949

Pupo Walker, C.Enrique. 'Los de abajo' y la pintura de Orozco: un caso de correspondencias estéticas. *Cuadernos Americanos.* 26(5):237-253; 1967

Renau, José. José Clemente Orozco, ein grosser Maler Mexikos. *Bildende Kunst.* 401-408; 1966

Reed, Alma. Orozco and Mexican painting. *Creative Art.* 9(3):198-207; September 1931

Rich, Daniel Catton. Orozco festival in Mexico. *Art News.* 46(3):15-17; May 1947

Rivas, Guillermo. José Clemente Orozco. *Mexican Life (Mexico).* 11(10):26-29; October 1935

Schmeckebier, Laurence. The frescoes of Orozco. *Mexican Life (Mexico).* 9(3); 1933

Schmeckebier, Laurence. The frescoes of Orozco in the New School for Social Research. *Trend.* 1(2); June 1932

Schmeckebier, Laurence. Orozco's graphic art. *Print Collector's Quarterly.* 21(2):185-94; April 1934

Scott, David. W. Orozco's Prometheus. *College Art Journal.* 17(1):2-18; Fall 1957

Soto Segarra, Luis de. El 'Museo Taller José Clemente Orozco.' *Arquitectura (La Habana).* 20:132-139; 1952

Spratling, William P. Orozco. *Mexican Life (Mexico).* 5(10):25-30; 1929 October 1929

Sweet, F. A. Leader, Zapata. *Chicago Art Institute Bulletin.* 35:89-91; November 1941

Tablada, José Juan. José Clemente Orozco, the Mexican Goya. *International Studio.* 78(322): 492-500; March 1924

Thwaites, John Anthony. The early works of Orozco. *Art Quarterly.* 7(2):76-89; 1944

Thwaites, John Athony. José Clemente Orozco and direct art. *Art Quarterly.* 8:83-98; 1945

Tietze, Hans. José Clemente Orozco als Graphiker. *Graphischen Kunste (Vienna).* 56(4):75-82; 1933

Tietze, Hans. Der mexikanische Maler, José Clemente Orozco. *Die Kunst* (Munich). 67:138-46; February 1933

Valle Heliodore, Rafael. Diálogo con José Clemente Orozco. *Universidad (México).* 2(11):22-23; diciembre 1936

Valle Heliodore, Rafael. José Clemente Orozco, entrevista. *Revista de Revistas (México).* septiembre 1935

Venezia: José Clemente Orozco celebrato alla Biennale. *Emporium.* 111:227-228, 1950

Villaurrutia, Xavier. José Clemente Orozco y el horror. *Romance (México).* 1(1):1,7; 10 febrero 1940

Watson, J. New commission for Orozco, Dive Bomber painted at the Museum of Modern Art. *Magazine of Art.* 33:434; July 1940

Werner, Alfred. Orozco: man of fire. *Arts Magazine.* 43(3):30-31; December 1968-January 1969

Westheim, Paul Orozco: een mexicaans fresco-schilder. *Kronick van Kunst en Kultuur.* 8(4):97-101; 1947

Yates, P. Tribute to a giant. *California Arts and Architecture.* 60:34; January 1943

Zadova, L. Iskusstvo Orosko. *Iskusstvo.* 23(10):37-45; 1960

Short List of General Books on the Mexican Mural Movement

Charlot, J. *The Mexican Mural Renaissance 1920-25,* London, 1963

Myers, B.S. *Mexican Painting in our Time,* New York, 1956

Schmeckebier, E.*Modern Mexican Art,* Minneapolis, 1939

Fondo de Cultura Económica *Mexican Mural Painting,* Mexico City, 1967

Rodriguez, A. *A History of Mexican Mural Painting,* London, 1969

Continued from p.59

20Reed, *ibid.*, pp.207-209. She says that '*In a salute to the arts, he placed at the table his favorite critic, Lloyd Goodrich, as a representative of the Anglo-Saxon world*' (i.e., second from left). Mr. Goodrich has a far more prosaic account of his inclusion: he had gone to watch Orozco (whom he had never met, but admired as an artist) paint one afternoon. Orozco had reserved a place for Alvin Johnson, who failed to appear, and asked Goodrich to pose for him since the plaster was on the verge of becoming too dry to paint (interview 17 April 1980).

21a. As Orozco notes in his **Autobiography** (p.127), Alma Reed met Carrillo Puerto in Yucatán while on assignment for the *New York Times*; they fell in love and planned to marry, but Carrillo Puerto — governor of Yucatán state at this time — was assassinated at the outbreak of the de la Huerta rebellion (1924).

b. According to Orozco (**Autobiography**, p.144), '**The Negro presiding and the portrait of Lenin were the occasion for the New School's losing a number of its richest patrons, a serious loss to an institution dependent upon gifts.**' Alvin Johnson, however, flatly denies this assertion: '*Although I lived with that picture for fifteen years I cannot say that I ever met or heard of a single person who withdrew one dollar on account of the mural*' (Johnson letter to Frank Rasky, newspaper reporter, dated 15 November 1949; from New School files).

c. Unfortunately, during the McCarthyite '50s (after Johnson had retired, I should add) the entire west wall was covered with a curtain. The New School stated (memo 'Answer to Questions About the Orozco Murals', dated 10 February 1953): '*It is the contents which make this particular section of the walls offensive to the legitimate feelings of too many people. Other aspects of the matter cannot justify the further display of this picture.*
The Board of Trustees has been considering a more permanent solution of the problem which is posed by the propagandistic intentions of Orozco's paintings and the prevailing opinion reacting to it.
The New School had not earlier bowed to opposition to the Soviet panel, lasting until the Soviet repulse of the German invasion during World War II, on the part of Trotyskites — 'the most violent critics' — and 'American conservatives, who were almost as bitter' (Johnson, *Notes . . . , p.12*).

22Orozco, **Autobiography**, p.144/149-50. 'Dynamic Symmetry' also concerns the 'Ashram', where Orozco met Hambidge's widow in 1928. Mary Hambidge, impressed with Orozco's grasp of Hambidge's system, proposed that he collaborate with her on work Hambidge left unfinished at his death, especially concerning the geometric construction of the human body (see Reed, *Orozco*, p.205).

23For Hambidge's ideas, see the periodical *The Diagonal* (1919-21).

24The paintings today are in appallingly deteriorated condition, as the pigment is literally flaking off the walls — the result of 50 years of neglect (the photos I have are from the time of painting). A Mexican restoration team examined the mural in 1974, and submitted these findings, which unfortunately were not acted on by New School authorities:
1. Severe damage from moisture, seeping in from the unsealed top floor (i.e., directly above the mural), and condensation inside the room.
2. The action of industrial pollutants through the years.

3. The brighter colors (blue, green) were applied in fresco secco *over the original* buon fresco painting, hence these sections are nowhere near as permanent.

25Octavio Paz interview in *Arts Canada*, December 1979-January 1980, nos. 232-233.

26Interview (22 April 1980) with Churchill Lathrop, art faculty member at the time and today Director Emeritus of Hopkins Center Art Gallery; it is largely due to his efforts and interest that the Dartmouth murals have remained in excellent condition since their painting. Prof. Lathrop also said that the Baker Library murals were only part of an envisioned mural program on the campus, and that other artists, such as Thomas Hart Benton were approached. Nothing materialized, however.

27a. Dartmouth College records, President Hopkins' file.

b. The original suggestion involving Orozco seems to have come from the Rockefeller family, substantial contributors to the College (Nelson was a member of the Dartmouth class of 1930), as President Hopkins wrote at the time (letter of 31 May 1932):
. . . my original interest in Orozco arose from the suggestion of one of the wealthy patrons of the College that in our teaching of the various eras of art and the various cycles of art it seemed that the College ought to give something in the way of instruction about Mexican art and about mural painting, both of which could be combined in the person of Orozco.

c. The arrangement also permitted Orozco to travel to Europe in the summer of 1932, to make periodic trips to New York, and to retain preparatory studies for the mural.

28a. Hopkins letter, *ibid.*, p.2. Dartmouth, I should say, was founded in 1769 by Eleazar Wheelock for the education of Indians.

b. The enthusiams of the Art Department for the project is indicated by Hopkins' comment (*ibid.*):
I thereupon asked for a definite assurance in regard to the appropriateness, if any, of the development of the theme suggested, and the Art Department became somewhat irritated, saying that so far as that went anything that Orozco did would be desirable for the College to possess.

29On the actual working process, Gobin Stair, a member of the 1933 Dartmouth class and handyman to Orozco, recalls ('The Making of a Mural', in *Dartmouth Alumni Magazine*, February 1973):
Orozco prepared drawings ahead of time. For some faces and most hands he made the drawing full size and pressed the lines through on the wet plaster with a brush handle. He also perforated the paper and tamped dusted color through the holes, but he sometimes created the design directly on the wall. He was so confident that he did it any way he wanted to do it, and this still gives me the feeling of the immediacy of the painting. It is more noticeable in the later part — the east wing; the earlier painting is more studied.
Elsewhere Stair talks about 'endlessly' grinding the white lime used as the white and opaque paint.'

30Orozco quoted in Dartmouth College news release, 25 May 1932.

31Quetzalcoatl — 'The Plumed Serpent': *Quetzal* is bird; *coatl* snake, and *atl* water — was both a god and possibly an extraordinary actual 10th century Toltec ruler and cultural figure. As a god Quetzalcoatl created present day man and the food staple, maize. Among other attributes, he was god of the wind, of life, of morning and the planet Venus.

32a. Artemas Packard, chairman of the art faculty at the time, in *Orozco at Dartmouth: A Symposium*, The Arts Press, Hanover, NH, 1933, p.10.

b. The departure of the leader Quetzalcoatl, and his sacrifice for mankind, forms an obvious thematic parallel to the **Prometheus**, the contemporary rebels and leaders in the New School, and anticipate the treatment of this theme at Guadalajara (**Hidalgo**, the '**Man of Fire**'). According to one account of the myth, Quetzalcoatl's departure was caused by evil magicians; another says that the god Tezcatlipoca made Quetzalcoatl drunk and sexually incontinent. The account of the departure also varies; in one Quetzalcoatl committed self-immolation and returned as the morning star; in another he built a raft of serpents and sailed away. All versions agree that he was to return.

33Originally Orozco intended something far different, as indicated in a schematic sketch (from Baker Library archives) in the east wing painting, i.e., now **Cortes** through to **Gods of the Modern World**:
1. Implements of Agrarian Society: symbol of colonial culture.
2. Cortez and the Cross: symbol of white man's materialism and idealism. In the foreground founders, liberators, and builders of the New World.
3. Arts and Crafts of the white man.
4. Symbol of the hope of a 'Golden Age': figures of typical American idealists.
5. Forces working against the best interests of humanity in modern American civilization.
6. A modern prophecy: symbol of man of the future. Foreground a group of ideal types of American leadership.
7. Implements of industrial society: symbol of modern culture.

34Lewis Mumford, 'Orozco in New England, *New Republic*, October 1934, p.233.

35According to Thomas Beggs (interview 5 March 1980), Orozco confirmed his suspicions when they met in Claremont in 1936 that the group of academics contained caricatures of Pomona College, President Edmunds and Dean of Students Blaisdell (last two figures to the right). Further, when lecturing on Orozco at Claremont during this period Mr Beggs would ask audience members if they recognized well-known people, and '*they would spot and tell me, rather than me telling them.*'

36This group also differs greatly from Orozco's original intentions, which called for paintings of 'The Missionaries — Dartmouth College, Explorers, and Settlers.' From mural proposal in Orozco's hand, Baker College archives.

37Orozco's letter to a 'Mr Harris', dated 8 October 1933, Baker College archives.

Contents

Contributors

Laurance Hurlburt: Born 1937. Art Historian. Specialist subject: *Mexican Muralist movement.* At present researching book on the influence of the Mexican muralists in North America and exhibition on the Mexican mural movement for the Detroit Institute of Arts. Resident in Middleton, Winsconsin, USA.

Desmond Rochfort: Born 1949. Mural painter. Completed mural on the theme of the construction worker north wall of Royal Oak murals, London. 1978, spent three months in Mexico invited by INBA and the British Council to research mural movement. Resident in London.

Michael Nungesser: Born 1950. Art historian. Specialist subjects: 19th and 20th Century mural painting and modern realist art in Mexico and the United States. Resident in West Berlin.

Olav Münzberg: Born 1938. Author, critic, poet. Co-editor of review *Aesthetik und Kommunikation.* Teaches at Freie Universität, West Berlin. Resident in West Berlin.

James Findlay: Born 1943. Latin American archivist at the Library of the Museum of Modern Art, New York. He has researched widely in 20th-century Latin American Art and has advised on bibliographic purchasing in this field for the Museum.